Reference Shelf®

The Two Koreas

The Reference Shelf
Volume 91 • Number 1
H.W. Wilson
A Division of EBSCO Information Services, Inc.

Published by
GREY HOUSE PUBLISHING
Amenia, New York
2019

The Reference Shelf

The books in this series contain reprints of articles, excerpts from books, addresses on current issues, and studies of social trends in the United States and other countries. There are six separately bound numbers in each volume, all of which are usually published in the same calendar year. Numbers one through five are each devoted to a single subject, providing background information and discussion from various points of view and concluding with an index and comprehensive bibliography that lists books, pamphlets, and articles on the subject. The final number of each volume is a collection of recent speeches. Books in the series may be purchased individually or on subscription.

Publisher's Cataloging-In-Publication Data
(Prepared by The Donohue Group, Inc.)

Names: Grey House Publishing, Inc., compiler, publisher.
Title: The two Koreas / [compiled by Grey House Publishing].
Other Titles: Reference shelf / H.W. Wilson, a Division of EBSCO Information Services, Inc. ; volume 91, number 1
Description: Amenia, New York : Grey House Publishing, 2019. | Includes bibliographical references and index.
Identifiers: ISBN 9781642652185 (v. 91, no. 1) | ISBN 9781642652178 (volume set)
Subjects: LCSH: Korea (North)--History--Sources. | Korea (South)--History--Sources. | Korea (North)--Social conditions--21st century--Sources. | Korea (South)--Social conditions--21st century--Sources. | Korea (North)--Foreign relations--United States--Sources. | United States--Foreign relations--Korea (North)--Sources. | Korean Americans--History--21st century--Sources.
Classification: LCC DS902 .T96 2019 | DDC 951.9--dc23

Printed in Canada

Contents

3

The Korean Threat

4

The Current Summit Talks and What They Mean for the Future

5

Korean Americans

Preface

Land of Mountains and Streams

For the United States and allied nations, North Korea has long been a source of controversy and concern. In the spring and summer of 2018, North Korea again entered the public debate when news reports indicated that the nation had developed offensive nuclear capabilities and was rapidly approaching a state in which it could attack the United States directly. For decades, the United States and allies have attempted to prevent the escalation of North Korea's military, utilizing negotiation, economic sanctions, and even threats of military force, but to little avail. To better understand the North Korean controversy, it is useful to look at the history and bifurcated cultures of the Korean Peninsula, from the kingdoms that united the peninsula to the struggle for global ideological dominance that ultimately tore the nation into warring halves. From the economic importance of South Korea's bustling urban economies, to the constant threat of North Korea's fundamentalist conservatism, to the lives of transplanted Koreans in the United States and elsewhere, Korea's long and storied culture has left a deep impact on the world.

From One to Two

Korea is a land noted for its rugged mountains, with eight separate mountain ranges that include four volcanoes, one of which, Baekdu, remains active and erupted as recently as 1903. Korean society evolved within mountain valleys, and the dividing line of the mountain ranges enabled these communities to evolve in partial isolation, developing unique mythological, political, artistic, and linguistic characteristics.

Life within this unique Korean landscape gave rise to a rich shamanic tradition. Early Koreans produced an extensive body of literature now known as "seolhwa," or "tales," about wildlife, nature, and people, as well as anecdotal lessons that recorded important facets of ancient Korean life and culture. Because of the peninsula's geographic location, jutting out from the Asian mainland between China and Japan, Korean culture has long been influenced by these neighboring cultures. The languages of all three states share certain characteristics and there is likewise overlap in the structure of Japanese, Chinese, and Korean mythology. As Korean society evolved from hunter-gatherer communities to agricultural settlements and eventually to city states, Korea, Japan, and China also shared imported religious beliefs, most notably Indian Buddhism, which was first imported into China before spreading throughout Northeast Asia.[1]

The strategic and economically important geographic position of the Korean Peninsula also meant that neighboring Japan and China competed for influence within its evolving kingdoms. It was Chinese military assistance, in fact, that enabled one of Korea's early kingdoms to unify the peninsula under a single dynasty. China and Japan continued to compete for control of the peninsula into the twentieth century, and a Japanese invasion in 1910 ended Korea's centuries-old dynastic leadership. For decades, Koreans were oppressed under a brutal military dictatorship until, in World War II, the nation was liberated by Russia and the United States. Russia and the United States, however, had their own goals in Northeastern Asia, with both powers seeking to create a renewed Korea sensitive and responsive to their economic and military needs. The result was that the nation was split in two, with Russia cultivating a communist military dictatorship in the north, while the United States tried, unsuccessfully, to foster a democratic society in the south. The Korean War devastated both sides of the divided nation, leaving millions dead, hundreds of years of infrastructure and architecture decimated, and the remaining population forcibly divided, with many families ripped apart and prevented from unification in what became a nearly 70-year military impasse.[2]

From the Korean War (begun in the 1950s) to the present, Korea's two sides evolved in different ways. Though the South endured decades of military dictatorship, internal revolt in the 1980s brought about democratic and industrial reform. Coupled with South Korea's military and economic partnership with the United States and Europe, South Korea's reform period led to the development of a robust economy with essential ties not only to allied nations in Northeast Asia, but to the rest of the world as well. Meanwhile, North Korea's fundamentalist conservatism led to the evolution of an insular military state controlled by a single family since the World War II split. North Korea, burdened by limited economic opportunities and resources and plagued by poverty, evolved into what is essentially a military cult, in which nearly one fourth of all resources are dedicated to the military and every member of society is expected to donate their lives, if necessary, to ensure the continuation of the dictatorial regime.[3]

The Kims of the World

With over 50 million living in South Korea, over 25 million in North Korea, and more than 10 million individuals of Korean descent living around the world, the Korean people are a diverse group that have spread to and influenced many societies. Though Koreans are as diverse as any other population, their names belie this. Until the Joseon Dynasty (1392-1910), only wealthy aristocratic families in Korea used surnames (also known as family or "last names"). When the practice of adopting surnames was first implemented, individuals registering with the government could choose their own family names, and it became common for individuals to purchase forged documents to grant their family a surname from a wealthy clan or noble house, thus increasing their stature. As a result, the surnames Kim, Lee, and Park—all derived from royalty—became nearly ubiquitous in Korean culture. In South Korea, nearly half of all citizens are named Kim, Park, or Lee; the surname Kim alone accounts for nearly 20 percent of the 50 million South Koreans.[4]

It is one of Korea's many Kims who is arguably the most famous Korean in the world: Kim Jong-Un, the much-maligned dictator currently leading the North Korean state. North Korea, officially known as the Democratic People's Republic of Korea, or DPRK, has, in fact, been led *only* by three generations of the Kim family, beginning with Kim Il-Sung, then passing to his son Kim Jong-Il, and finally, in 2010, to North Korea's most recent chairman, Kim Jong-Un. From the end of the Korean War, the North Korean military has sought to develop nuclear weapons. The United States has been North Korea's most dangerous enemy since North Korea fought US and allied soldiers in the Korean War. As the United States used atomic weapons against Japan at the end of World War II, the DPRK regime feared that they might eventually opt for a similar strategy in their goal to exert US control within Northeast Asia. Meanwhile, the United States and the international community have been using economic sanctions since the end of the Korean War as a way to prevent the DPRK from gaining military strength. These sanctions have, over decades, limited the growth of the DPRK and are part of the reason that North Korea in 2019 has achieved only a fraction of the economic growth and global significance as its southern counterpart.[5]

Russia, allied with North Korea during the Korean War, helped the nation start its nuclear program in the 1950s. In the decades since, nearly every presidential administration in the United States has taken some action toward addressing the threat of nuclear proliferation in Asia. Frequently, these efforts take the form of additional trade or economic sanctions intended to either limit North Korea's ability to obtain materials or to limit the growth of the economy. In general, all efforts to stop North Korea from developing nuclear weapons have failed because none of the negotiating nations were prepared to use military force or invasion to eliminate the nation's weapons-development programs. The DPRK leadership, in turn, has been unwilling to end their weapons program in return for economic agreements alone. As the United States and allies have nuclear capabilities and stronger militaries, since the first Kim dynasty in North Korea the DPRK position has been that its nuclear weapons program is the only military development initiative with the potential to protect the nation from invasion.[6]

Summiting It Up

By 2018, North Korea's controversial weapons tests had proved that the nation had successfully developed nuclear weapons, though the extent of its arsenal remained unclear. Pronouncements from the DPRK's official propaganda department elicited a response from the Trump administration, alternating between insults and diplomatic overtures. This resulted in the first meeting between a US president and a North Korean chairman since the Carter administration, but it did not result in a substantive peace agreement or specific plans for disarmament. The Trump administration thus faces the same situation faced by past US leaders, an intransigent regime that refuses to disarm unless the United States removes military threats from Northeast Asia and significantly eases sanctions against North Korea.

In the months since Donald Trump and Kim Jong-Un began trading threats and insults, journalists, political analysts, and politicians have either been critical of the Trump administration's hostile strategy, or expressed hope that the Trump government might take a harder line with the DPRK than past presidents have been willing to. Up for debate as well has been the nature of the North Korean threat. While some view Kim Jong-Un as capable and perhaps willing to use nuclear weapons offensively, some national security experts believe that such measures would be taken only if another foreign power attempts an invasion or a takeover of the North Korean government. Outside of the threat of direct military confrontation, some worry that North Korea's weapons program could lead to the Kim government dealing nuclear weapons or technology to rogue states or terrorist groups. Others have expressed concern that North Korea's cyber warfare capabilities have reached a stage at which the nation poses a significant threat to the US economy and potentially to US military technology as well.

Entering 2019, it remains unclear what role the United States will play in North Korea's continuing evolution.

However, 2018 brought about a series of unexpected changes between North and South Korea that some hope signifies a new beginning for the long-opposed nations. After meetings between Kim Jong-Un and South Korean president Moon Jae-in, the two nations released statements describing a series of joint ventures that included demilitarizing the border between the two nations and creating stronger economic agreements. In December, it was announced that work had begun on a rail line to unite the two sides of the peninsula. After years of tense relations, announcements from both the North and South indicate a willingness to discuss the long-awaited and perennially controversial issue of reunification.[7]

As with future meetings between the United States and North Korea, it is unclear what these renewed negotiations between the North and South will accomplish. What is clear, is that both North and South Korea are changing, and both nations are seeking deeper and stronger connections with the world around them. If the momentum achieved in 2018 can be maintained moving forward, it is possible that Korea could begin working toward a reunited society, if not under a single government or leader, than at least close enough that Koreans on both sides could reclaim some facet of what their ancestors experienced when their nation was whole.

Works Used

Choe, Sang-Hun. "North and South Korea Set Bold Goals: A Final Peace and No Nuclear Arms." *The New York Times*. The New York Times Co. Apr 27, 2018. Retrieved from https://www.nytimes.com/2018/04/27/world/asia/north-korea-south-kim-jong-un.html.

Cumings, Bruce. *Korea's Place in the Sun*. New York: W. W. Norton & Company, 2005.

"Factbox: History of Failure: Efforts to Negotiate on North Korean Disarmament." *Reuters*. Reuters. Mar 6, 2018.

Hwang, Kyung Moon. *A History of Korea*. New York: Palgrave Macmillan, 2017.

La Shure, Charles. "Korean Mythology." *Pantheon*. Encyclopedia Mythica. Sep 29, 2018. Retrieved from https://pantheon.org/articles/k/korean_mythology.html.

"Nuclear." *NTI*. Nuclear Threat Initiative. Oct 2018. Retrieved from https://www.nti.org/learn/countries/north-korea/nuclear/.

"Why So Many Koreans Are Called Kim." *The Economist*. The Economist Newspaper. Sep 9, 2014. Retrieved from https://www.economist.com/the-economist-explains/2014/09/08/why-so-many-koreans-are-called-kim.

Notes

1. La Shure, *"Korean Mythology."*
2. Hwang, *A History of Korea*.
3. Cumings, *Korea's Place in the Sun*.
4. "Why So Many Koreans Are Called Kim," *The Economist*.
5. "Nuclear," *NTI*.
6. "Factbox: History of Failure: Efforts to Negotiate on North Korean Disarmament."
7. Choe, "North and South Korea Set Bold Goals: A Final Peace and No Nuclear Arms."

1
A Tale of Two Koreas

By National Palace Museum, via Wikimedia

Seventh-century Tang dynasty painting of the envoys from the Three Kindoms of Korea: (left to right) Baekjae, Goguryeo, and Silla. The three kingdoms were unified when China's Tang Dynasty helped the Silla kingdom conquer its rivals around 668 CE.

Hanguk and Choson

The name Korea, sometimes poetically translated as the "Land of High Mountains and Sparkling Streams," refers to two separate nations, born of the same cultural roots but subject to diverging political and economic forces. United until the Japanese invaded the peninsula during World War II, the history of Korea has since been dominated by the political aims of the global superpowers. While South Korea evolved into one of the most affluent nations in Asia, North Korea developed into a totalitarian regime marginalized by decades-long poverty and limited personal or political freedom.

For the Korean people, the ongoing division within Korea remains a source of frustration and sadness. Families forced apart during the Korean War have remained divided due to the ongoing political rivalry between the two states. Over the years since the split, the cultures of the two nations have diverged to the point that South Koreans and North Koreans now use different terms when referring to their shared peninsula. South Koreans frequently use Hanguk, roughly translating to "great country," while North Koreans use the term Choson, a reference to one of the ancient dynasties of the nation's past.

According to the Asia Society, Koreans use a proverb—"When whales fight, the shrimp's back is broken"—to refer to the history of their country, reflecting how the Korean people have been repeatedly victimized by the struggles of more powerful countries.[1]

Land of Ancient Kingdoms

The Korean Peninsula is a large landmass extending 1,100 kilometers (683 miles) south along the eastern edge of the Asian mainland. In South Korea, it has become popular to describe the continent as shaped like a tiger, which is both an ancient symbol of good fortune in Korean culture and also conjures images of the fierce and powerful economy the nation wishes to create. Before the division of the Koreas, it was more common to describe the peninsula as having the shape of a rabbit, which symbolizes both wisdom and tradition.

Surrounded on three sides by water, the Korean Peninsula has 8,458 kilometers of coastline (5,255 m) and comes into contact with five separate bodies of water, the Sea of Japan, the Yellow Sea, the Korea Strait, the Cheju Strat, and the Korea Bay. Nearly 70 percent of the peninsula is mountainous, interspersed with arable plains between mountain ranges, and so agriculture has been confined to only a small portion of the peninsula. Mountains and streams are such an iconic part of the peninsula's geography that these features have become ubiquitous in Korean art.

In terms of natural resources, both the North and South are blessed with vast mineral wealth, a benefit of living within a rocky, mountainous terrain. Although governmental mismanagement and a lack of infrastructure has largely prevented North Korea's regimes from taking advantage, it has been estimated that the North Korean landscape harbors trillions in mineral resources, including gold, iron, zinc, copper, limestone, molybdenum, and graphite, which are only some of the 200 minerals and rare earth metals present in the nation's landscape.[2] Outside of mineral wealth, both nations have extensive coastal territories sitting alongside once resource-rich waters, and seafood has played a major role in the evolution of Korean society.

The highest mountains lie in the northern part of the peninsula, the largest being the volcano known as Baekdu Mountain, which extends some 2,744 meters (9,000 ft) above sea level and sits on the border of North Korea and China. Baekdu last erupted in 1903 but remains active. In the south, the peninsula extends into a series of more than 3,500 islands stretching into the surrounding seas, some of which are occupied but most of which are relatively barren and windswept bastions for sea birds and other migrants.

The Korean climate varies widely between north, south, east, and west. In the south, warmer temperatures prevail because of a warm air current, whereas the northern part of the country receives wind passing over the tundra of Siberia. The entire peninsula is within a monsoon zone, with monsoon rains and violent storms common in the summer.[3] Once hosting a diverse assemblage of plants and animals, over-development and warfare decimated animal populations across the country and have left vast portions of the peninsula environmentally degraded. In modern Korea, a number of threatened animals disappearing from the settled regions of the countries have taken shelter in the Demilitarized Zone (DMZ), a 155-mile strip dividing North and South Korea that has been forbidden to human traffic since the unofficial end of the Korean War (in 1953) and so has provided an unintended refuge for wildlife like the white-naped and red-crowned cranes, both of which are endangered but also treasured symbols of Korea's imperial legacy.[4]

Archaeologists have found evidence of agricultural settlements from as early as 5,500 years ago, when Korean farmers were already cultivating millet, soy, and beans. Records indicate that these settlements had a complex written language and indicate also a rich mythology. The mytho-poetic history of the peninsula, as a political entity, can be traced back to the legendary figure Dangun Wanggeom, sometimes known as Tangun, who is credited in popular myth as the founder of the Gojoseon kingdom, or "Ancient Joseon" period. Though historians doubt the existence of an actual Dangun, generations of Korean rulers have claimed to have descended from Dangun's lineage as a way to claim spiritual predetermination for their leadership. Dangun is often depicted as a shaman-king, and some historians speculate that the personage of Dangun was invented to symbolize the transition from the Stone Age to the Iron Age. Over the centuries, the Dangun legend continued to influence Korean politics and society in numerous ways. The location of the modern North Korean capital of Pyongyang, for instance, was chosen because it was the legendary site of the first city of Dangun's unified peninsula.[5]

Unification of the Three Kingdoms

The earliest clan communities that occupied the peninsula formed small towns and communities consisting of multiple towns, which then evolved into tribal leagues, and eventually into kingdoms. The earliest kingdom identified by archaeologists and historians was Goguryeo, which evolved from a loose confederation of tribes around 37 BCE and formed a powerful riparian kingdom along the Yalu River. At the height of this kingdom's power, it controlled most of the modern Korean Peninsula as well as portions of what is now southern China and a small portion of Russia. The southern portion of the peninsula was, at that time, split between two other kingdoms, known as the Baekjae (or Paekche) and the Silla. Historians therefore commonly refer to this part of Korean history as the Three Kingdoms period.

Competition between the three kingdoms ended when China's Tang Dynasty backed the Silla Kingdom, which then conquered its rivals in the north and south to unify the peninsula around 668 CE. The Chinese Academy of Social Science (CASS), a government-funded research institution, concluded that the Goguryeo kingdom had not been an independent kingdom but rather a satellite state of the Chinese Empire, thus suggesting that the earliest Korean kingdom was of Chinese making and not a product of ethnic Korean invention. The South Korean press coverage of the CASS studies soured South Korean attitudes toward the Chinese, with Korean politicians and academics claiming that China was attempting to erase the nation's unique cultural identity through an act of historical appropriation. In the 2000s, this led to a spate of historical dramas on South Korean television and in theatres depicting fictionalized versions of the Three Kingdoms period in which the Korean identity of the Goguryeo kingdom is retained. Though the extent of the reaction in North Korea is unknown to the US press, both South and North Koreans are known to have incorporated Goguryeo cultural artifacts and history into their national identities.[6]

Despite China's attempts to appropriate Korean history, there is little doubt that China, Japan, and Korea have had tremendous influence on one another since before the Goguryeo period dawned. The Korean written language has absorbed elements of Chinese and Japanese and all three nations share religious traditions as well. For much of Korea's dynastic history, the state cult was Buddhism, which was originally invented in India but was later imported into China, where it flourished and gave rise to a number of unique Chinese versions of the philosophy. From there, Buddhism was imported to Korea, where it further evolved before it was eventually exported to Japan. The relationship between the East Asian powers has therefore long been one of both competition and cultural exchange.

The Silla Kingdom that rose to first unify Korea began to deteriorate due to internal strife, and a former Silla general, Wang Geon, formed his own kingdom in the south. In 935, the king of the Silla Kingdom surrendered his thrown, enabling the Goryeo to take control of the entire peninsula. Wang Geon chose his own home town, Songak (now known as Gaeseong), as the capital of his new kingdom and set about fostering modernizations that made the Goryeo Dynasty among the most sophisticated in all of Asia. A wealth of art and architecture and Buddhist literature speak of the complex intellectual side of the Goryeo, which also supported an impressive scientific tradition. It was Goryeo inventors who created movable metal type printing in 1234, nearly two centuries before Germany's Gutenberg made the same discovery. Among the lasting artifacts of the kingdom is a series of more than 80,000 wooden blocks carved with the entire Buddhist canon, now stored in the Haeinsa Temple in South Korea.

It was also during the Goryeo Dynasty period that Korea first had contact with Muslim traders traveling the Silk Road. These traders carried stories and artifacts from the Goryeo into India and the Middle East and eventually to Europe. It was the Goryeo Dynasty that gave the peninsula its modern English and European name as the name of the dynasty was transliterated to become Korea.

The Goryeo Dynasty began to crumble in the 1200s due to a combination of internal power struggles and external pressure. This left the kingdom vulnerable to Mongolian invasions, which began in the early 1200s and turned the Goryeo into a vassal state under long-distance Mongolian dominance. In 1392, another military coup toppled the Goryeo and installed a new dynasty, known as the Joseon, under the leadership of former general Yi Seong-gye. Embracing Chinese Confucianism, the Joseon state was guided by a class and caste system based on civil service and stressing the importance of education, and the Joseon became a powerful and culturally innovative kingdom. The reign of King Sejong the Great, from 1418 to 1450, produced an artistic and scientific renaissance that left behind an invaluable wealth of textiles, sculpture, and scientific artifacts.

Foreign Influence

For centuries, a military alliance between Korea and China, in return for exports from Korea, protected the nation from more powerful neighbors, though this protection was, at times, insufficient. Japanese forces invaded Korea in the sixteenth century and the Manchurian armies also invaded in the seventeenth century, after invading China as well. These repeated invasions made the Korean kingdom increasingly insular, so much so that nineteenth-century scholars called Korea a "Hermit Kingdom." Korea first opened the nation to diplomatic relations only in 1876, under increasing pressure from Japan, and Japan, China, and Russia were the chief competitors seeking to use a strong alliance with Korea to strengthen their military and trade position in Northeastern Asia. After fighting both China and Russia between 1895 and 1905, Japan became the preeminent power in East Asia. In 1910, Japan annexed Korea and ruled the nation for 35 years under a military regime, attempting to force Koreans to abandon their language and cultural identity. In 1939, the Japanese took this forced assimilation further when they instituted a system that forced Koreans to adopt Japanese names.[7]

The Japanese colonial period was transformative, introducing many modern industries such as steel, cement, and chemical manufacturing to Korea during the 1920s and 1930s. Though the occupational government was brutal and exploitative, it left Korea as the second-most technologically advanced nation in Asia, behind only Japan itself. The fate of the Koreas shifted with the end of World War II and the surrender of Japan to the allies. As it was the United States and the Soviet Union that jointly accepted the Japanese surrender of Korea, both nations agreed to occupy roughly half of the country, with the Soviet Union occupying the territory north of the 38th parallel and the United States occupying the southern half.

The initial agreement between the United States and Russia was that the occupation would last only long enough for a unified government to be established and a new constitution implemented, but rising tensions between the United States and Russian leaders exacerbated ambitions among regional leaders in the two sides of Korea. In the summer of 1948, this breakdown in negotiations resulted in the establishment of two governments, one in Seoul, backed by the United States, which became the Republic of Korea (ROK), and another in Pyongyang, supported by the Soviet regime, which became the Democratic People's Republic of Korea (DPRK). With both governments claiming to be the legitimate representative of the entire peninsula, the political stalemate worsened until, in 1950, the DPRK, backed by soviet forces, invaded the south with the aim of forced unification. The United States and United Nations forces intervened to support South Korean independence, resulting in a devastating three-year war.

The Korean War was one of the greatest tragedies of the twentieth century, resulting in millions of lost lives and dozens of cities, towns, and entire communities destroyed. By 1953, the opposing forces had reached a stalemate, resulting in a ceasefire and the establishment of the DMZ, which is still in place in 2019. In fact, though the ceasefire has held since it was established, no official end to the war was ever declared. In the decades since, South Korea evolved into a technologically and socially advanced state, flourishing through its trade and cultural connections to the broader international community. North Korea, on the other hand, remained a nation deeply dominated by their military and its authoritarian power. In the twenty-first century, roughly one quarter of North Korea's budget is spent on military development, the highest proportion of any world nation. For some South and North Koreans, the question of reunification still looms, especially for those with long-estranged families across the heavily militarized border, but the long political impasse between the two nations has made this a remote possibility.

For many Americans living in the twenty-first century, America's fraught relationship with North Korea may be perceived as little more than the troubling process of attempting to curb the potentially dangerous aspirations of a dictatorial state, but this perspective ignores America's role in creating both North and South Korea. The fate of all those nations impacted or shaped by America's Cold War conflict is also part of America's legacy. How the United States handles its relations with North and South Korea is therefore more than simply a reflection of global politics.

Works Used

Armstrong, Charles K. "Korean History and Political Geography." *Asia Society*. Center for Global Education. 2018. Retrieved from https://asiasociety.org/education/korean-history-and-political-geography.

Billock, Jennifer. "How Korea's Demilitarized Zone Became an Accidental Wildlife Paradise." *Smithsonian*. Smithsonian Institution. Feb 12, 2018. Retrieved from https://www.smithsonianmag.com/travel/wildlife-thrives-dmz-korea-risk-location-180967842/.

Cartwright, Mark. "Dangun." *Ancient History Encyclopedia*. Oct 20, 2016. Retrieved from https://www.ancient.eu/Dangun/.

"The History of Korea." *UCC*. University College Cork, Ireland. 2018. Retrieved from https://www.ucc.ie/en/asian/research/asi/korean/factsaboutkorea/thehistoryofkorea/.

Mollman, Steve. "North Korea Is Sitting on Trillions of Dollars of Untapped Wealth, and Its Neighbors Want In." *QZ*. Quartz Media. Jun 15, 2017. Retrieved from https://qz.com/1004330/north-korea-is-sitting-on-trillions-of-dollars-on-untapped-wealth-and-its-neighbors-want-a-piece-of-it/.

Nemeth, David J. "The Geography of the Koreas." *Asia Society*. Center for Global Education. 2018. Retrieved from https://asiasociety.org/education/geography-koreas.

Washburn, Taylor. "How an Ancient Kingdom Explains Today's China-Korea Relations." *The Atlantic*. The Atlantic Monthly Group. Apr 15, 2013. Retrieved from https://www.theatlantic.com/china/archive/2013/04/how-an-ancient-kingdom-explains-todays-china-korea-relations/274986/.

Notes

1. Armstrong, "Korean History and Political Geography."
2. Mollman, "North Korea Is Sitting on Trillions of Dollars of Untapped Wealth, and Its Neighbors Want In."
3. Nemeth, "The Geography of the Koreas."
4. Billock, "How Korea's Demilitarized Zone Became an Accidental Wildlife Paradise."
5. Cartwright, "Dangun."
6. Washburn, "How an Ancient Kingdom Explains Today's China-Korea Relations."
7. "The History of Korea," UCC.

Why Is the U.S. Wary of a Declaration to End the Korean War?

By Edward Wong
The New York Times, August 13, 2018

WASHINGTON—As a reward for its broader foray into diplomacy, North Korea wants a formal and official declared end to the decades-long Korean War that settled into an uneasy truce in 1953. South Korea wants this, too.

But the United States, which first sent military forces to the Korean Peninsula in 1950 and still keeps 28,500 troops there, is not ready to agree to a peace declaration.

No doubt the issue will be high on the agenda when the leaders of the two Koreas hold their third summit meeting next month, in Pyongyang. Both want the end of the war to be declared this year with the United States and, possibly, China. And North Korea insists on securing the declaration before moving forward with denuclearization.

But there is a range of reasons American officials have refused so far to embrace a formal peace declaration. The Trump administration wants North Korea to first halt its nuclear weapons program—a tough line that could create a divergence between the United States and South Korea, its ally.

In turn, analysts said, that gives an opening to North Korea—and maybe China and Russia—to exploit the gap between Washington and Seoul.

"You have South Korea moving so quickly on these projects to push for reconciliation with North Korea, and in Washington you have people pushing for denuclearization before anything else happens," said Jean H. Lee, director of the Wilson Center's center for Korean history and public policy. "They have very different end games and very different time frames. It's very problematic."

First, the U.S. Wants Proof of Pyongyang's Efforts to Denuclearize

The Trump administration, like those of Presidents Barack Obama, George W. Bush and Bill Clinton, is focused on North Korea's nuclear weapons program above all else. That's in large part because North Korea has been developing an intercontinental ballistic missile that would give Pyongyang the ability to strike the United States mainland with a nuclear warhead.

> **Although a peace declaration is not the same as a binding peace treaty, it would start the process for one.**

In a joint statement released after the Singapore summit meeting in June, the United States and North Korea said Pyongyang "commits to work toward complete denuclearization of the Korean Peninsula."

But the two sides didn't agree on the definition of denuclearization.

For President Trump's top foreign policy officials—Mike Pompeo, the secretary of state, and John R. Bolton, the national security adviser—denuclearization means North Korea halting and dismantling its nuclear weapons program.

Mr. Bolton said last week that North Korea had not taken steps necessary for denuclearization, a process that American officials have said should include turning over a list of Pyongyang's atomic weapons stockpiles, nuclear production facilities and missiles.

North Korea has not agreed to do so and, according to Mr. Pompeo, is still producing fissile material at plants. Separately, American intelligence officials have concluded that North Korea is continuing to make long-range missiles at a site north of Pyongyang, according to news reports.

South Korea wants the United States to give Kim Jong-un, the North Korean leader, something significant—ideally an end-of-war declaration—to build domestic political will for denuclearization.

South Korean officials also have noted that North Korea is focused on the order of points made in the joint statement from Singapore. The commitment to denuclearization was third, while the first and second points called on the United States and North Korea to establish new relations and to build "a lasting and stable peace regime on the Korean Peninsula."

For the North Koreans, that means prioritizing an end-of-war declaration and peace treaty, analysts said.

Joseph Y. Yun, the former senior diplomat on North Korea at the State Department, said in an interview that Washington and Pyongyang could try for a "declaration-for-declaration" agreement: North Korea would declare its nuclear assets in exchange for the United States' supporting a declaration to end the Korean War.

The Two Koreas Want a Declaration by This Fall—Way Too Soon for the U.S.

For the declaration, the two Korean governments are working on a year's end deadline at the latest, but ideally by the Sept. 18 start of the annual United Nations General Assembly meeting in New York. It is widely believed that United Nations officials might invite Mr. Kim to attend the assembly and deliver a speech.

"The best-case scenario is that Kim Jong-un visits the United Nations with a peace declaration in hand," said John Delury, a professor at Yonsei University in Seoul who writes on the Korean conflict and Chinese history.

The Koreas had originally considered putting together an end-of-war declaration in July, but that did not happen.

Given their skepticism over North Korea's commitment to denuclearization, American officials said the timeline was much too fast.

As always, the wild card is Mr. Trump. He insisted that the Singapore summit meeting be held in June, even though American officials wanted more time to prepare.

Mr. Trump might aim for a similar foreign policy extravaganza in the fall, timed to the United Nations assembly and before the crucial November midterm elections in the United States.

American Officials Worry a Peace Declaration Could Dilute the U.S. Military in Asia

Although a peace declaration is not the same as a binding peace treaty, it would start the process for one. That would mean talking about how many American troops are needed in South Korea. Before the Singapore meeting, Mr. Trump ordered the Pentagon to prepare options for drawing down the troops there now.

For some American officials, the troop presence in South Korea is not just a deterrent toward North Korea. It also helps the United States maintain a military footprint in Asia and a grand strategy of American hegemony.

China has already begun challenging the United States' military presence in Asia, which will only be reinforced as China becomes the world's biggest economy and modernizes its military.

The officials also worry that President Moon Jae-in of South Korea might try to push for a lesser American military presence, or a weakening of the alliance, after an end-of-war declaration.

"For the United States, an end-of-war declaration or a peace treaty has always had a broader context," Mr. Yun said.

Print Citations

CMS: Wong, Edward. "Why Is the U.S. Wary of a Declaration to End the Korean War?" In *The Reference Shelf: The Two Koreas*, edited by Micah L. Issit, 9-11. Ipswich, MA: H.W. Wilson, 2019.

MLA: Wong, Edward. "Why Is the U.S. Wary of a Declaration to End the Korean War?" *The Reference Shelf: The Two Koreas*, edited by Micah L. Issit, H.W. Wilson, 2019, pp. 9-11.

APA: Wong, E. (2019). Why is the U.S. wary of a declaration to end the Korean War? In Micah L. Issit (Ed.), *The reference shelf: The two Koreas* (pp. 9-11). Ipswich, MA: H.W. Wilson.

Why There Are Two Koreas

By Matthew Wills

JStor Daily, March 17, 2017

The two Korean states, which both claim to be the legitimate government of a divided Korean Peninsula, are in the news again. North Korea is testing missiles that could potentially carry nuclear warheads. South Korea is getting a new anti-missile system from the U.S. It is the latest in a long and tormented relationship between the neighboring states.

The Koreas were split at the end of WWII. That was when the Japanese, who annexed the peninsula in 1910, were replaced by occupying forces from the Soviet Union in the north and the United States in the south. The partition line at the 38th parallel would eventually mark the border of what have become vastly different countries.

The war of 1950-53, which involved more than a dozen countries under the aegis of the U.N. aiding the South, and China and the U.S.S.R. aiding the North, ended in an armistice that never evolved into an actual peace treaty. Since then tensions have simmered along the DMZ (demilitarized zone). The U.S., which provided the bulk of the U.N. force during the war, continues to station some 28,500 military personal in South Korea.

American involvement goes back further than WWII. For many Koreans, the Taft-Katsura memorandum of 1905 remains a contentious piece of their history and the U.S.'s role in it. Kirk W. Larsen and Joseph Seeley examine how popular depictions of this "secret treaty" reinforce North Korean suspicion of the U.S. and South Korean disappointment with the U.S.

The memorandum itself documented a conversation between U.S. Secretary of State William Howard Taft and Japanese Prime Minister Katsura Taro. It has been interpreted in the Koreas as an *agreement* about spheres of influence, with Japanese getting control of Korea and the U.S.

American involvement goes back further than WWII.

control over of Philippines. Few historians in the U.S. or South Korea subscribe to this reading, but, as the authors note, popular memory and perception "prefers clean, simple narratives that ostensibly speak to deeper truths" to the research and writing of scholars.

Another area of great debate is how the North, the Democratic People's Republic of Korea, actually came about. North Korea, where independent scholarship is not allowed, presents it all as guided by Kim Il Sung, the "Great Leader" (and grandfather of current leader Kim Jong-un). In South Korea and the U.S., the North was seen as a puppet state of the Soviet Union. Gwang-Oon Kim argues that it was a combination of, and contest between, both native and foreign influences.

The DPRK broke with the Soviet Union in the mid-1950s. Since then, the country's *juche* (self-reliance) ideology, essentially born in the cauldron of Japanese and then Soviet interference, has been one of hermetic self-sufficiency. This is why, Kim thinks, the isolated North Korean state handily survived the breakup of the U.S.S.R and the Warsaw Pact, as well as China's turn towards state-sponsored capitalism, and in fact, why it still exists today.

Print Citations

CMS: Wills, Matthew. "Why There Are Two Koreas" In *The Reference Shelf: The Two Koreas,* edited by Micah L. Issit, 12-13. Ipswich, MA: H.W. Wilson, 2019.

MLA: Wills, Matthew. "Why There Are Two Koreas" *The Reference Shelf: The Two Koreas,* edited by Micah L. Issit, H.W. Wilson, 2019, pp. 12-13.

APA: Wills, M. (2019). Why there are two Koreas In Micah L. Issit (Ed.), *The reference shelf: The Two Koreas* (pp. 12-13). Ipswich, MA: H.W. Wilson.

Korean War a "Forgotten" Conflict That Shaped the Modern World

By Liam Stack

The New York Times, January 1, 2018

The Korean War has been called "the Forgotten War" in the United States, where coverage of the 1950s conflict was censored and its memory decades later is often overshadowed by World War II and the Vietnam War.

But the three-year conflict in Korea, which pitted communist and capitalist forces against each other, set the stage for decades of tension among North Korea, South Korea and the United States.

It also helped set the tone for Soviet-American rivalry during the Cold War, profoundly shaping the world we live in today, historians said.

As tensions between North Korea and the United States continue to mount amid missile tests and taunts, here is a brief guide to the Korean War and the impacts that linger more than 60 years after its end.

How Did the Korean War Start?

The Korean War began when North Korean troops pushed into South Korea on June 25, 1950, and it lasted until 1953. But experts said the military conflict could not be properly understood without considering its historical context.

Korea, a Japanese colony from 1910 until 1945, was occupied by the United States and the Soviet Union at the end of World War II. The United States proposed temporarily dividing the country along the 38th Parallel as a way to maintain its influence on the peninsula, which bordered Russia, said Charles K. Armstrong, a professor of Korean history at Columbia University. A divided Korea was something unprecedented," he said.

But the divide lasted in part because of competing visions among Koreans for the country's future. "Fundamentally it was a civil war, fought over issues going back into Korea's colonial experience," said Bruce Cumings, a professor of history at the University of Chicago.

In 1948, the American-backed, anti-communist southern administration, based in Seoul, declared itself the Republic of Korea. It was led by Syngman Rhee, who lived in exile in the United States for many years and was installed as the South

Korean leader by the Office of Strategic Services, a predecessor to the Central Intelligence Agency, Professor Cumings said.

Soon after, the Soviet-backed, communist northern administration, based in Pyongyang, declared itself the Democratic People's Republic of Korea. Its leader was Kim Il-sung, who fought alongside communist forces during the Chinese civil war and was the grandfather of North Korea's current dictator, Kim Jong-un.

> **South Korea did not agree to the armistice, and no formal peace treaty was ever signed.**

Each regime was unstable, rejected the legitimacy of the other and considered itself to be Korea's sole rightful ruler. Border skirmishes between the two were frequent before the Korean War began.

Who Were the Combatants?

The war pitted South Korea and the United States, fighting under the auspices of the United Nations, against North Korea and China.

Other nations contributed troops, too, but American forces did most of the fighting. "The South Korean Army virtually collapsed" at the start of the war, Professor Cumings said.

The Soviet Union supported North Korea at the beginning of the war, giving it arms, tanks and strategic advice. But China soon emerged as its most important ally, sending soldiers to fight in Korea as a way to keep the conflict away from its border.

The Chinese leader, Mao Zedong, also saw China's participation in the war as a way to thank Korean Communists who fought in the Chinese civil war, Professor Cumings said.

"There was a lot of field contact between American and Chinese forces," Professor Armstrong said. "In a sense, this was the first and only war between China and the United States, so far."

How Damaging Was It?

The war devastated Korea. Historians said that between three million and four million people were killed, although firm figures have never been produced, particularly by the North Korean government. As many as 70 percent of the dead may have been civilians.

Destruction was particularly acute in the North, which was subjected to years of American bombing, including with napalm. Roughly 25 percent of its prewar population was killed, Professor Cumings said, and many of the survivors lived underground by the war's end.

"North Korea was flattened," he said. "The North Koreans see the American bombing as a Holocaust, and every child is taught about it."

Damage was also widespread in South Korea, where Seoul changed hands four times. But most combat took place in the northern or central parts of the peninsula around the current Demilitarized Zone, which divides the countries, Professor Cumings said.

How Did It End?

Technically, the Korean War did not end.

The fighting stopped when North Korea, China and the United States reached an armistice in 1953. But South Korea did not agree to the armistice, and no formal peace treaty was ever signed.

"There is still a technical state of war between the combatants," Professor Cumings said.

Neither North nor South Korea had achieved its goal: the destruction of the opposing regime and reunification of the divided peninsula.

Since 1953 there has been an uneasy coexistence between North and South Korea, which hosts over 20,000 American troops. At one time hundreds of American nuclear weapons were based there.

"It was from the Korean War onward that we had a permanent, global American military presence that we had never had before," Professor Armstrong said. Other countries that host American troops include Qatar, Japan, Italy and Germany. "It was a real turning point for America's global role."

In the decades after the war, South Korea transformed into an economic powerhouse. Professor Cumings said many of its citizens now know little about the conflict and have "a fatalistic orientation" toward the economically isolated North.

Meanwhile, North Korea became "the world's most amazing garrison state with the fourth largest army in the world."

"Its generals are still fighting the war," Professor Cumings said. "For them it has never ended."

Print Citations

CMS: Stack, Liam. "Korean War, a 'Forgotten' Conflict That Shaped the Modern World." In *The Reference Shelf: The Two Koreas,* edited by Micah L. Issit, 14-16. Ipswich, MA: H.W. Wilson, 2019.

MLA: Stack, Liam. "Korean War, a 'Forgotten' Conflict That Shaped the Modern World." *The Reference Shelf: The Two Koreas,* edited by Micah L. Issit, H.W. Wilson, 2019, pp. 14-16.

APA: Stack, L. (2019). Korean War, a "forgotten" conflict that shaped the modern world. In Micah L. Issit (Ed.), *The reference shelf: The Two Koreas* (pp. 14-16). Ipswich, MA: H.W. Wilson.

History of US-North Korea Deals Shows Hard Part Is Making Them Stick

By Julian Borger
The Guardian, June 11, 2018

It is Donald Trump's recurring boast that with the Singapore summit with Kim Jong-un, he has succeeded in negotiations with North Korea where his predecessors failed. But the claim obscures a long history of agreements made and broken by both countries.

The lesson of two major deals, in 1994 and 2005, is that it is much easier to reach agreements than to implement them. In fact, the complex, fraught process of implementation has usually brought with it new flashpoints and new crises.

Trump's looming Singapore summit with Kim will be the first meeting between US and North Korean leaders, but that is largely because previous US presidents have balked at giving the Pyongyang regime such recognition and prestige without substantive progress towards disarmament.

Each time a deal has been close, the same basic bargain has been on the table: that North Korea relinquish its nuclear arsenal in return for a mix of security and economic incentives.

In 1992—the first time the US and North Korea engaged diplomatically since the 1953 armistice—the Pyongyang regime faced similar isolation and intense economic pressure as it does today. The collapse of the Soviet Union robbed the regime of a steadfast ally and patron. Meanwhile, Beijing was telling North Korea to undergo the same transformative economic reforms as China. Kim's grandfather, Kim Il-sung, was facing an existential threat.

Then, like now, rapprochement between North and South Korea created a diplomatic opening for the US. In January 1992, the two Koreas signed an agreement on the denuclearisation of the Korean peninsula. That led to meetings between American and North Korean diplomats at the US mission to the United Nations in New York, where the two delegations eyed each other warily after three decades of silence.

The first thing that struck Robert Gallucci, who became chief US negotiator in 1993, was his counterparts' identical lapel badges portraying the Great Leader. "I tried to imagine us sitting there with lapel pictures of Bill Clinton and I just couldn't," he recalled.

The first two years of US engagement with North Korea were highly volatile, in which diplomatic breakthroughs were interspersed by dangerous crises.

North Korea made an agreement in January 1992 with the International Atomic Energy Agency (IAEA) to allow its nuclear complex at Yongbyon to be inspected, and at the same time the US called off its joint military exercises with South Korea.

The consequent mood of optimism was short-lived. The arrival of the IAEA inspectors led rapidly to a conflict on how much of the Yongbyon nuclear plant they could see. The escalation culminated in the North Koreans unloading spent fuel rods from the Yongbyon reactor, a necessary precursor to extracting plutonium. The Clinton administration started reviewing plans for air strikes to stop them and the two sides came close to war.

Just before Washington got to the point of ordering the evacuation of US nationals from the peninsula, the former president Jimmy Carter stepped in. He flew to Pyongyang for a personal meeting with Kim Il-sung, putting the diplomacy back on track and providing the impetus for the first major accord between the two countries, the 1994 Agreed Framework.

According to the deal, North Korea would dismantle its reactor at Yongbyon, the source of its plutonium, in return for two civilian light water nuclear power stations, generally seen as less of a proliferation risk. Until those reactors were built, North Korea would receive shipments of US-financed fuel oil.

The deal was sealed in Geneva and the North Koreans invited the US negotiators to their mission to toast its success. One of the US diplomats, Joel Wit, was on the point of downing his shot when he spotted snakes at the bottom of the bottle. It was snake liquor, popular across east Asia for special occasions.

"Snake liquor really does smell like there has been a dead animal in the bottle, because there is," Wit said. "I didn't drink it, and as I turned around to put the glass down on the table I noticed that all the other Americans put theirs away. I'm not sure if the North Koreans noticed."

From such tentative beginnings, the Agreed Framework would last nearly nine years, but its implementation would be a constant struggle. A Republican-dominated Congress did its best to slow down fuel deliveries, and the construction timetable for the reactors was continually postponed.

It later emerged that North Korea had been cheating by pursuing a secret uranium route to making a bomb. That was enough for the hawks in the Bush administration, John Bolton among them, to kill off the Agreed Framework.

The accord's defenders suggest that the uranium enrichment programme was the regime's hedge against the US reneging on the deal, and it could have been closed down through negotiations. They also argue that the Agreed Framework held back the weapons programme for most of the 1990s.

Christopher Hill, who became the Bush administration's chief negotiator with North Korea, disagreed with the decision to end the Agreed Framework. "My own view is we lost control of the plutonium process, we lost inspectors on the ground. We lost the capacity to understand what was going on there," Hill said.

After a break in contact of more than two years, Hill was given the task of re-establishing contacts with the North Koreans under the format of multilateral, six-party talks. Those negotiations eventually led to a 2005 joint statement of principles to guide future negotiations, which included some of the elements of the Agreed Framework, such as the eventual provision of light water reactors, and a lot of language that will be on the table in Tuesday's talks between Trump and Kim.

The statement called for "the verifiable denuclearization of the Korean Peninsula ... in a phased manner in line with the principle of 'commitment for commitment, action for action.'"

The joint statement once more raised hopes that the US and North Korea had turned a corner in their relationship, but it began to fall apart almost immediately. Within weeks, the US Treasury imposed new sanctions, freezing $23m (£17m) in North Korean assets in a bank in the Chinese territory of Macau, using counter-terror legislation. It was a relatively small amount of money, but it infuriated the North Koreans and the Chinese, who saw it as a violation of the spirit of the joint statement. US diplomats who had negotiated the 2005 statement were also taken by surprise.

"I think it's fair to say that one part of the US government was not particularly in touch with another part of US government, not for the first or last time," said Hill, who saw it as an act of sabotage by hawks such as Bolton in the Bush administration. "I think the real purpose of it was to screw up the negotiations."

As relations spiralled downwards, North Korea tested seven ballistic missiles in July 2006, and conducted its first nuclear test in October the same year.

The US ended up refunding North Korea the money it had frozen in Macau, and provided shipments of fuel oil, and in return the regime closed down its Yongbyon reactor and provided a partial inventory of its nuclear programme. But the six-party talks became bogged down in the question of verification. As before, North Korea was prepared to allow inspectors in but sought to limit what they could see.

> **Each time a deal has been close, the same basic bargain has been on the table: that North Korea relinquish its nuclear arsenal in return for a mix of security and economic incentives.**

Kim Jong-un has struck one deal with the US, in February 2012. Under the Leap Year agreement, the regime undertook once more to suspend enrichment in Yongbyon under IAEA verification and to suspend nuclear and missile testing, in exchange, the Obama administration pledged to send food aid.

Once more, the deal fell apart within weeks when North Korea conducted missile launches, which it insisted were for satellite deployment. The US deemed them a breach of the Leap Year agreement and halted plans to send food aid.

Through three generations of the Kim dynasty, and successive US administrations, the biggest obstacle has not been reaching an agreement but making it stick. This has not only been a result of North Korea seeking to circumvent deals it has made, but a recurrent problem of US administrations sending conflicting signals, as different factions vie for control of policymaking.

Whatever form of words Trump and Kim Jong-un agree on Tuesday, the history of US negotiations with North Korea suggest an agreement on paper is just the start, not the end, of any effort to achieve a real compromise.

Print Citations

CMS: Borger, Julian. "History of US-North Korea Deals Show Hard Part Is Making Them Sick." In *The Reference Shelf: The Two Koreas,* edited by Micah L. Issit, 17-20. Ipswich, MA: H.W. Wilson, 2019.

MLA: Borger, Julian. "History of US-North Korea Deals Show Hard Part Is Making Them Sick." *The Reference Shelf: The Two Koreas,* edited by Micah L. Issit, H.W. Wilson, 2019, pp. 17-20.

APA: Borger, J. (2019). History of US-North Korea deals show hard part is making them sick. In Micah L. Issit (Ed.), *The reference shelf: The two Koreas* (pp. 17-20). Ipswich, MA: H.W. Wilson.

US.-ROK: The Forgotten Alliance

By Kongdan Oh
Brookings Institution, October 13, 2008

Most stories about Korea in the news media are about *North* Korea (the Democratic People's Republic of Korea or DPRK). The Six-Party Talks seeking an end North Korea's nuclear weapons program are not going well. Severe food shortages continue. North Koreans are caught in smuggling and counterfeiting operations. And on the country's 60th anniversary, its dictatorial leader, Kim Jong-il, fails to make an appearance, strengthening rumors that he is severely ill.

But *South* Korea (the Republic of Korea or ROK) is of much greater importance to the United States. Its gross national income is 35 times larger than North Korea's, and its trade volume 240 times greater. South Korea has been a member of the OECD group of economically successful nations since 1996, and is today America's seventh largest trading partner. In 2008, South Korea also is celebrating its 60th anniversary, and in October, the 40th Security Consultative Meeting (SCM) between the U.S. and ROK secretaries of defense, which receives little press coverage. The first SCM (under a different name), was held in March 1968 to coordinate defense strategy against North Korea, which two months earlier had captured the *USS Pueblo* and launched a commando raid against the ROK presidential mansion (the Blue House).

The U.S.-ROK Mutual Defense Treaty, signed in October 1953, two months after the end of the Korean War, has guaranteed South Korea's national security. The security alliance counts as one of the most important of America's alliances, not only serving to deter another North Korean attack on South Korea, but also providing a continental base for U.S. forces to face China and Russia and to provide a front-line defense for Japan. The alliance has also augmented South Korea's military forces and provided a nuclear umbrella, thus enabling the South Koreans to pursue economic progress with relatively low military budgets.

> **The U.S.-ROK Mutual Defense Treaty, signed in October 1953, two months after the end of the Korean War, has guaranteed South Korea's national security.**

Like other security alliances, the U.S.-ROK alliance is easily overlooked during peacetime. It is sometimes viewed as more of a burden than a benefit, considering the shared cost of keeping troops stationed in Korea and the imposition, if you will, of having foreign troops stationed in one's country—an experience Americans are not familiar with. Sometimes the presence of American forces has triggered large protests, most notably in 2002 when a large American armored vehicle accidentally crushed two fourteen-year-old Korean girls walking along the side of a country road.

Emotions eventually cooled after that horrific event, and apologies were belatedly offered, but issues of contention continue to bedevil the alliance. The U.S. Forces in Korea (USFK) have agreed to vacate their large base in downtown Seoul and relocate to the countryside, but the two countries disagree on how to share the enormous costs of the move. As the USFK consolidates its operations, other bases are closing, with debates about how much responsibility the United States bears for cleaning up the land before handing it over to the original owners.

Print Citations

CMS: Kongdan, Oh. "U.S.-ROK: The Forgotten Alliance." In *The Reference Shelf: The Two Koreas,* edited by Micah L. Issit, 21-22. Ipswich, MA: H.W. Wilson, 2019.

MLA: Kongdan, Oh. "U.S.-ROK: The Forgotten Alliance." *The Reference Shelf: The Two Koreas,* edited by Micah L. Issit, H.W. Wilson, 2019, pp. 21-22.

APA: Kongdan, O. (2019). U.S.-ROK: The forgotten alliance. In Micah L. Issit (Ed.), *The reference shelf: The two Koreas* (pp. 21-22). Ipswich, MA: H.W. Wilson.

2
Life in the Two Koreas

The DMZ Train, or Peace Train, is a South Korean tourist attraction that runs along a restored rail line formerly used to connect North and South Korea. Passengers travel from Seoul to Dorastan Station, the terminal closest to the DMZ, and North Korea. The symbolic journey embodies the hope of future reunification.

Lives Divided

Though the two sides of Korea were united for millennia, over the nearly 70 years since the Korean War, the northern and southern sides of Korea have evolved in increasingly divergent ways. South Korea's evolution was deeply influenced by the nation's long-standing political and economic alliances with the United States and Western Europe, developing into a complex and affluent consumer culture, while North Korea has been ruled by a single dynasty of military leaders, the Kim family, who have utilized social and political repression to create a military-based state cult. The two Koreas provide an example of how cultural evolution occurs when embracing at least some degree of globalism, as in the case of South Korea, or when embracing isolationism, as is the case in the DPRK.

The Land Between

Many North and South Koreans living in the twenty-first century have no direct memory of Korean life before the North/South split. Between the two societies lies the Demilitarized Zone (DMZ), a 380-square-mile strip of land littered with landmines and bordered on both sides by fences, border walls, and other armaments. Decades of abandonment have transformed the area into an unintentional preserve where many rare Korean animals, like musk deer, cranes, martens, Eurasian lynx, and Asiatic black bears, survive even as they have been largely eliminated from the more populous parts of both nations.[1] Amidst this dangerous, yet strangely thriving, wilderness, there is a single village: Taesung, also called "Freedom Village," the only South Korean settlement within the zone. The village sits just 500 yards from the border of North Korea and is home to a peculiar population of 197 villagers, a movie theatre, and a single restaurant.

Life in Taesung provides an interesting look at the ideological war still being conducted across the DMZ. Villagers are never out of earshot of a constant stream of propaganda pumped through loudspeakers arrayed along the North Korean side of the DMZ. South Korea's speakers are likewise always blaring, but typically stream news and occasionally even pop music to counter the drone of state-propaganda from the north. Taesung's villagers must live with the constant reminders of the tensions between the two nations. When they travel into or out of South Korea, for instance, they must do so under armed guard, a precaution against kidnapping, of which there have been several instances impacting the village over the past decades.[2]

Nowhere is North and South Korea's mutual distrust more evident than in the Joint Security Area (JSA), also known as Panmunjom Truce village, where North and South soldiers stand armed, face-to-face, ready to attack on command. Former US President Bill Clinton called the JSA the "scariest place on earth," but it has begun to change since the days of the Clinton administration's efforts to broker a more harmonious peace between the two sides. In October 2018, South Korean president Moon Jae-in and North Korean leader Kim Jong Un signed a historic disarmament agreement wherein both parties agreed to remove landmines and weaponry from the JSA, followed by three-party inspections (through the United Nations) to ensure that both sides had honored the agreement. In joint statements, Moon and Kim vowed to turn the entire JSA into a "Peace Zone."[3]

Southern Hospitality

While South Korea has a culture very different from that of the United States, it is a culture with which citizens of the United States can easily relate. Since dividing from North Korea after World War II, the evolution of South Korea has been deeply influenced by the nation's connections to the international community. After the separation, South Korea passed through a difficult and tumultuous political transformation. A military coup led by General Park Chung-hee in 1961 resulted in the establishment of a military dictatorship. Social and political conditions deteriorated to the point that the entire population was placed under martial law in 1972. After Park was assassinated in 1979, control passed to General Chun Doo-Hwan, and another military dictatorship. Despite the continuing dictatorship, South Korea's international alliances enabled the nation to retain at least some level of gradual technological and industrial advancement and the military regime slowly relinquished authority under pressure from anti-dictatorship dissidents. In 1987, a student-led movement forced Chun from power and this eventually led to the 1993 elections in which Kim Young Sam, a dissident and outspoken critic of the military regime, became the first freely-elected president, marking a shift to representative democracy.[4]

Since transitioning away from dictatorship, the South Korean economy has grown rapidly, making the nation one of the most powerful economic forces in Northeast Asia. With over 5.4 million citizens, South Korea has also become an increasingly metropolitan society, with more than 80 percent of the nation's 5.4 million citizens living and working in one of the nation's growing urban metropolises.[5] Ethnographic studies have shown that South Korea has developed an unusually strenuous professional and work culture, which is a product of traditionalist values that place emphasis on hard work as an indicator of personal and familial value. A 2017 study from the Organization for Economic Cooperation and Development (OECD) indicated that South Koreans are among the hardest working in the world, working an average of 2,069 hours per year, which is second only to Mexico, where the nation's chronically overworked and underpaid population work an average of 2,225 hours each year. By comparison, though US citizens sometimes view themselves as unusually hard working, Americans average 1,783 hours per year, which is far closer to the global average. South Koreans also earn less per hour, on average, than their counterparts in other developed countries and thus sociologists have noted that extreme stress and poor work/life balance has become characteristic of South Korean daily life.[6]

On the artistic and recreational levels, South Korea has also developed features that set the nation apart. South Korea's cities have become famous for an aggressive culture of recreational options, including late-night video-game arcades, virtual reality cafes, overnight spas, exotic animal cafes where visitors can interact with wild animals, and even features like "rage rooms," where customers can spend time smashing objects, throwing knives or axes, or engaging in a number of other destructive activities meant to help the population defuse stress. Music is at the center of South Korean culture and the nation's home-grown genre, known as K-pop, features outrageous fashion, dance routines, and a focus on theatrical value and spectacle and has become one of the few music genres not invented in the United States to achieve true global appeal, with K-pop concerts, fan groups, and imitators springing up in the United States and across Europe. For citizens, music is an essential part of recreational culture as well, with karaoke being one of the most popular forms of entertainment. Cities like Seoul have 24-hour party districts, typically located near universities, where citizens young and old can engage in year-round carnival entertainment.[7] Sociological studies of South Korea indicate that the aggressive, obsessive recreational culture of South Korean cities is the counterweight to the nation's work-obsessed and stress-filled professional environment.

Although South Korea has a rich artistic culture, it is far less diverse than many other of the world's metropolitan societies. Nearly 40 years of isolation under the nation's military regimes mean that more than 99 percent of South Korean citizens are ethnic Korean. The lack of cultural diversity can be seen in the homogeneity of South Korean art and other features of society. For instance, few religions are represented with the religious population generally split into either Buddhism (24.4 percent) or Protestant Christianity (24 percent), but with few other faiths represented. This feature of South Korean society is also eroding, with more than 45 percent of the country, according to some polls, claiming no religion.

Further, the lack of diversity has fed into one of South Korea's most pressing social issues, demographics marked by a gender imbalance and falling birth rate. This feature is, in part, related to traditionalist ideals in which South Korean families focused on males, and often aborted female births. The median age in Pyeongchang is expected to reach 60 by 2045, making it one of the oldest societies in the world, the result of a society in which there is barely one child born per woman, combined with rising life expectancy. Economists predict that this demographic system will devastate the South Korean economy over the next half century, due to a labor shortage and the cost of caring for an aging population. The government has offered free fertility treatment, economic child care bonuses, and other incentives, but without result. Some economic experts have suggested that South Korea must create an easy immigration path for migrant workers and refugees, helping to bolster population numbers while also contributing to the diversity of the nation's culture.[8]

Northern Soul

In many ways, it is impossible for Western scholars to accurately compare and contrast the cultures of South and North Korea, as there is insufficient information available about North Korea. The North Korean Communist Party took control of the nation in 1948, with Kim Il-Sung, first patriarch of the Kim dynasty, installed as lifetime leader of the government. The failed invasion of South Korea in 1950—the Kim regime's attempt at forced reunification—resulted in millions of lives lost across both sides but no gains for North Korea. Since the armistice, the Kim family has remained in power, jealously safeguarding their dynastic dominance through a strict system of social and political controls. As South Korea made the transition to representative democracy, North Korea remained locked in conservative totalitarianism.

The gradual normalization of relations between North Korea and other world nations began slowly in the 2000s and accelerated after Kim Jong-Il (son of Kim Il-Sung and the second of the Kim dynasty to lead North Korea) suffered a stroke that eventually led to his replacement by son Kim Jong-Un in 2010. Under all three generations of the Kim family, nuclear development has been a key factor in the nation's continued isolation within the international community, resulting in limited trade and thus persistent poverty and a lack of resources within the DPRK.[9]

Over the years, North Korea has developed a reputation for being one of the most isolationist and secretive societies in the world. North Korea has philosophically embraced its isolation from the global community by promoting the philosophy of "iuche" or "self-mastery," the idea being that there is virtue in the North Korean people relying only on themselves. This philosophy was promoted by Kim Il Sung and used as the justification for enforced cultural isolation and the need for a strong national defense system, which has completely dominated the North Korean economy and culture since.[10]

What little is known about life inside North Korea comes from rare journalistic visits and from defectors who have illegally crossed the border into South Korea or traveled to the United States, Europe, China, or elsewhere. Investigative reports suggest that the Kim regime invests heavily in creating a cult-like allegiance to both the Kim dynasty and to the nation's military. Investigators who have gained a rare glimpse behind this curtain have described a society that is, in many ways, dysfunctional. For instance, journalist Barbara Demick, who interviewed escaped North Koreans for her 2009 book, *Nothing to Envy*, said of the society, "In the futuristic dystopia imagined in *1984*, George Orwell wrote of a world where the only color to be found was in the propaganda posters. Such is the case in North Korea." What escapees have described is a world entirely shaped by constant government propaganda. There is one newspaper and one television station, both controlled by the state and both only producing material that celebrates the Kim dynasty and filters any global news in such a way as to validate and even heroically characterize the state's actions.

The Kim dynasty has also shaped society so as to celebrate and glorify the Kim family itself. Reporter Suki Kim, who spent six months undercover in North Korea in 2011, told *CNN* reporters that "to try to understand North Korea, it's basically a cult of the great leader. It's a military dictatorship with one of the largest armies in the world and also it's a place where communication is blocked." Kim went on to describe a building in one North Korean city dedicated to studying the "great leader" Kim, where citizens go both to study the leader but also to guard and clean the building in order to show their allegiance. Residents were allowed only one newspaper, and one television station. However, Kim also said of her experience that the North Korean people were "lovely and absolutely human," but existed within an emotionally and intellectually isolated bubble.[11]

Official educational materials provided to children within the society contend that the Kim family's leadership is part of a divine directive for the development of their society. In some cases, stories of the Kim family's greatness may even appear like petty boasting. The propaganda network has, for instance, claimed that Kim scored a perfect 300 the first time he went bowling, and shot five holes-in-one the first time he played golf. In 2012, state media outlets reported the discovery of a kirin den, a mythical animal allegedly ridden by Tongmyong, the mythopoetic founder of Korea. The discovery was meant to reinforce the alleged legitimacy and divine nature of the Kim family's leadership by connecting their version of Korea to the historic founding of the nation.[12] Though the Kim family promotes its own divine connection, studies indicate that there is little in the way of active religion within the nation, which is another part of the cult-creation program, not only promoting religious affiliations with the leading class, but also replacing other forms of community and organization, like religion, with allegiance and adherence to the state.

In many ways, North Korea is even more culturally homogenous than its Southern neighbor and this homogeneity has also become part of the propagandistic message of the ruling organs of the state. The degree to which there is internal dissent is unclear, but there are indications that the power of the Kim dynasty is beginning to fade, especially among the younger generation. The more recent softening of relations between the north and south may indicate that the Kim dynasty recognizes this erosion and the need to embrace at least some degree of integration with the international community.

Works Used

Hancocks, Paula and Taehoon Lee. "Checkpoints, Curfews and Barbed Wire: Life in the Village on North Korea's Doorstep." *CNN*. CNN. Sep 5, 2017. Retrieved from https://www.cnn.com/2017/09/05/asia/south-korea-dmz-village/index.html.

Hancocks, Paula, Kwon, Jake, and Joshua Berlinger. "North, South Korea Begin Demilitarizing 'Scariest Place on earth.'" *CNN*. CNN. Oct 25, 2018. Retrieved from https://www.cnn.com/2018/10/25/asia/north-south-korea-dmz-intl/index.html.

Kasulis, Kelly. "South Korea's Play Culture Is a Dark Symptom of Overwork." *QZ*. Quartz Media. Dec 31, 2017. Retrieved from https://qz.com/1168746/south-koreas-play-culture-is-a-dark-symptom-of-overwork/.

Larmer, Brook. "South Korea's Most Dangerous Enemy: Demographics." *The New York Times Magazine*. Feb 20, 2018. Retrieved from https://www.nytimes.com/2018/02/20/magazine/south-koreas-most-dangerous-enemy-demographics.html.

Mahtani, Melissa. "North Korea Is 'a Cult' to Kim Jong Un, Undercover Reporter Says." *CNN*. CNN Politics. Aug 12, 2017. Retrieved from https://www.cnn.com/2017/08/12/politics/undercover-reporter-north-korea-cult-cnntv/index.html.

"North Korea Profile—Timeline." *BBC News*. BBC. June 13, 2018. Retrieved from https://www.bbc.com/news/world-asia-pacific-15278612.

Pappas, Stephanie. "7 Strange Cultural Facts About North Korea." *Live Science*. Purch. Apr 8, 2013. Retrieved from https://www.livescience.com/28528-7-cultural-facts-north-korea.html.

Quinn, Ben. "Unicorn Lair 'Discovered' in North Korea." *The Guardian*. The Guardian News and Media. Nov 30, 2012. Retrieved from https://www.theguardian.com/world/2012/nov/30/unicorn-lair-discovered-north-korea.

Se-hwan, Bak. "South Koreans Work Second-Largest Hours in OECD for Below Average Pay." *The Korea Herald*. The Korea Herald Corporation. Aug 17, 2017. Retrieved from http://www.koreaherald.com/view.php?ud=20170816000716.

"South Korea—Timeline." *BBC News*. May 1, 2018. Retrieved from https://www.bbc.com/news/world-asia-pacific-15292674.

Szczepanski, Kallie. "South Korea—Facts and History." *ThoughtCo*. DotDash. Aug 21, 2017. Retrieved from https://www.thoughtco.com/south-korea-facts-and-history-195724.

Yoon, Dasl and Andrew Jeong. "If You Think North Korea Is a Wild Place, Check Out the DMZ." *The Wall Street Journal*. Dow Jones & Company. Dec 3, 2018. Retrieved from https://www.wsj.com/articles/cranes-vs-cranes-korean-dmz-development-poses-a-test-for-conservation-1543762801.

Notes

1. Yoon and Jeong, "If You Think North Korea Is a Wild Place, Check Out the DMZ."
2. Hancocks and Lee, "Checkpoints, Curfews and Barbed Wire: Life in the Village on North Korea's Doorstep."
3. Hancocks, Kwon, and Berlinger, "North, South Korea Begin Demilitarizing 'Scariest Place on Earth.'"
4. "South Korea-Timeline," *BBC*.
5. Szczepanski, "South Korea—Facts and History."
6. Se-hwan, "South Koreans Work Second-Longest Hours in OECD for Below Average Play."
7. Kasulis, "South Korea's Play Culture Is a Dark Symptom of Overwork."
8. Larmer, "South Korea's Most Dangerous Enemy: Demographics."
9. "North Korea Profile—Timeline," *BBC News*.
10. Pappas, "7 Strange Cultural Facts About North Korea."
11. Mahtani, "North Korea Is 'a Cult' to Kim Jong Un, Undercover Reporter Says."
12. Quinn, "Unicorn Lair 'Discovered' in North Korea."

These Are the Only People Who Live Inside the DMZ between North and South Korea

By Thomas Maresca
USA Today, April 25, 2018

TAESUNG VILLAGE, South Korea—At first glance, this tiny village looks like an ordinary farming community in rural South Korea. Rice fields, tractors and modest homes dot the landscape. There's a church, an elementary school, even a tiny movie theater.

But life for Taesung's 207 residents is anything but ordinary. They're the only people living inside the Demilitarized Zone, the buffer area 160 miles long and 2.5 miles wide that has divided the peninsula since the end of the Korean War in 1953.

South Korean soldiers escort farmers to and from their fields every day to steer them clear of landmines inside what is often called the most heavily guarded border in the world.

Just 440 yards away is the demarcation line that separates North and South Korea, and beyond that is the North Korean town of Kijong, a seemingly uninhabited "propaganda village" featuring an imposing 525-foot-high flagpole, one of the world's tallest.

As leaders from Seoul and Pyongyang prepare for Friday's historic summit, few will watch more closely than the residents of Taesung. Mayor Kim Dong-ku said the recent period of détente between the North and South has made a noticeable difference in the village.

"Since we're so close to North Korea, we feel very nervous when the tensions are high," he said. "Due to the talks, the atmosphere has gotten much better."

Perhaps the most striking change has been in the noise level. North Korea usually blasts a non-stop stream of propaganda songs and speeches from loudspeakers inside Kijong but agreed to turn off the sonic assault this week ahead of the summit. South Korea also stopped playing K-pop tunes, news and information from its own high-powered loudspeakers on the border.

"The propaganda stopped (on Monday)," Kim said. "It's much more relaxed here now."

Living under such conditions may seem hard to imagine, but Taesung also has its benefits. Farmers here are given rights to a 17-acre plot of land per family and typically earn $80,000 to $100,000 a year, far more than the average South Korean farmer.

They also don't pay federal taxes since the village is under United Nations Command, and men are exempt from South Korea's mandatory military service.

Like Mayor Kim, almost all the residents of Taesung—also called Freedom Village—are natives. The only way anyone can move into the town is if a woman marries a local man. Inhabitants are required to spend 240 days a year in Taesung.

Beyond a sporadically open movie theater located inside the town hall, there are no shops or businesses inside Taesung. Residents can come and go through the heavily fortified barriers and checkpoints of the

Most of the young people in the village have ambitions beyond Taesung.

DMZ into nearby South Korean towns and cities such as Paju, but a curfew is in effect from midnight until 5 a.m.

Taesung does have an elementary school—with 35 students from pre-kindergarten to sixth grade—and inside the well-kept building, the shadow of tensions with North Korea seems distant. Colorful student artwork decorates the walls. And laughs and shouts from the children reverberate through the hallways during break times.

One banner turns this unusual location inside the DMZ into a positive affirmation: Dream Making Zone, it reads.

Facing a shrinking town population, the school allowed children from outside the village, and they now account for 27 of the 35 students. They are drawn here by high-tech facilities, no tuition and the unique bonus of English lessons with volunteer U.S. soldiers stationed inside the DMZ.

The students practice emergency drills at least twice a year, said school principal Jin Young-jin, and they aren't allowed off the campus during the school day. But the principal said the students are unperturbed by their unusual circumstances.

"The children aren't afraid," he said.

The bigger threat Taesung faces may not be from the North, but from the same forces draining small towns and farming communities all over the world: the lure of the big city. South Korea is a heavily urbanized country, with more than 80% of people living in cities. About half of the country's 51 million residents are concentrated in the capital, Seoul.

Mayor Kim said he hopes that the upcoming inter-Korean summit will bring a lasting atmosphere of peace to the village. But he noted that most of the young people in the village, including his own two school-age children, have ambitions beyond Taesung.

"There's not much to do here other than farming," Kim said. "My children want to move to the city when they're old enough."

Print Citations

CMS: Maresca, Thomas. "These Are the Only People Who Live Inside the DMZ between North and South Korea." In *The Reference Shelf: The Two Koreas,* edited by Micah L. Issit, 31-33. Ipswich, MA: H.W. Wilson, 2019.

MLA: Maresca, Thomas. "These Are the Only People Who Live Inside the DMZ between North and South Korea." *The Reference Shelf: The Two Koreas,* edited by Micah L. Issit, H.W. Wilson, 2019, pp. 31-33.

APA: Maresca, T. (2019). These are the only people who live inside the DMZ between North and South Korea. In Micah L. Issit (Ed.), *The reference shelf: The two Koreas* (pp. 31-33). Ipswich, MA: H.W. Wilson.

What Is Life Like for South Korean Kids? Busy

By Hau Chu
The Washington Post, January 23, 2018

You might not give people on the other side of the world much thought because you figure that their lives are a lot different from yours.

As the Winter Olympics in PyeongChang approaches, however, you might wonder what life is like for kids in South Korea. The answer: very busy.

While a typical school day can be tough for students in America, the educational culture in South Korea can make it seem like a breeze.

"I had a lot of pressure from school, education-wise, like a typical Korean household," said Jackie Yoo, 25, who was born in America but moved with her family to South Korea at age 4 and remained there through high school.

"From first grade, I remember having a math tutor after school, and then straight after that I would have a piano lesson and then ballet, so there was a lot of pressure outside of school education—which was a bit stressful," she said.

In addition to regular school, many parents enroll their kids in a private tutoring service called a hagwon (HAH-gwon). Children attend school and then go to a hagwon for studying.

"In America, we'll have tutoring. Maybe if you're not so good at math or not so good at Spanish, you'll have one to three hours of tutoring," said Jason Bartlett, 24, a graduate student at Georgetown University in Washington, D.C., who studied in South Korea during college and later worked there as a tutor.

"In Korea, parents will sign their kids up for years to go to these hagwons for English, for math—even if they're very good. It's not just because they're struggling, it's because they want their child to be the best, to excel and not fall behind."

Hagwons became so popular that kids sometimes stayed until the middle of the night. The South Korean government responded with a curfew: No hagwon could stay open after 10 p.m.

The most popular reason for enrollment is preparation for the Suneung (SOON-ung), the college entrance exam. It's not uncommon for preschoolers to be enrolled in a hagwon that prepares kids for this test while teaching other skills.

Kids also learn English from a young age, but those lessons can be fun, Yoo said.

"Instead of growing up with traditional Korean movies, a lot of times at school we would watch foreign movies in English so that we can learn," she said.

Yoo said her young cousins in South Korea became hooked on *Frozen* after seeing it at school.

But kids' lives in South Korea aren't all about school. Like American children, South Ko-

> **While a typical school day can be tough for students in America, the educational culture in South Korea can make it seem like a breeze.**

reans entertain themselves with smartphones. About 72 percent own one by age 12, according to a 2016 report in the journal *Computers in Human Behavior*. Most use a free messaging service called KakaoTalk (KAH-cow talk), or KaTalk for short, to communicate.

"We don't use text messages. We use that app because we can message each other back with free phone calls and video calls," Yoo said.

One hot topic of conversation on KakaoTalk and in the lunchroom is Korean pop, more commonly known as K-pop. Korean boy bands and girl groups are hugely popular. At the top of the heap is BTS, a seven-member boy band with more than 8 million Instagram followers.

K-pop fans are interested in much more than the music. They are obsessed with pop-star gossip and style, Yoo said.

"Kids are always up-to-date with their fashion, music, hairstyle, hair color and even the color of the contacts that K-pop singers have in their eyes."

South Korea by the numbers

Size: 38,500 square miles, or slightly smaller than Virginia.
Population: 51.2 million, or about six times Virginia's population.
Biggest city: Seoul, 9.8 million people.
Currency: Won—$1 equals 1,069 won.
Fun fact: At birth, South Korean children are considered 1 year old. And everyone turns a year older on January 1. So if you were a South Korean born in mid-December, you would be considered 2 years old when an American child would be only 2 weeks old.

Print Citations

CMS: Hau, Chu. "What Is Life Like for South Korean Kids? Busy." In *The Reference Shelf: The Two Koreas*, edited by Micah L. Issit, 34-35. Ipswich, MA: H.W. Wilson, 2019.

MLA: Hau, Chu. "What Is Life Like for South Korean Kids? Busy." *The Reference Shelf: The Two Koreas,* edited by Micah L. Issit, H.W. Wilson, 2019, pp. 34-35.

APA: Hau, C. (2019). What is life like for South Korean kids? Busy. In Micah L. Issit (Ed.), *The reference shelf: The two Koreas* (pp. 34-35). Ipswich, MA: H.W. Wilson.

For South Korea's LGBT Community, an Uphill Battle for Rights

By Elise Hu
NPR, July 25, 2017

South Korea is one of the world's richest nations, a modern place with trends changing as fast as its Internet speeds. But when it comes to some social issues, the country has been slow to change—especially for gays and lesbians.

While there are shows of support—this month, a record 85,000 people turned up at Seoul's annual pride festival, for example—recent events indicate South Korea's institutions and political class are only reluctantly tolerating sexual minorities.

"We have to get more sexual minorities to vocalize their opinions and feel safe to come out of the closet," said theater actor Lee Sang-hoon, a gay man who goes by the stage name Summer.

His troupe was in the parade and dressed in lingerie for a skit at its booth. It was one of the 110 exhibitors at Seoul's pride fest, which was—as in previous years—protected by barriers and lines of police.

It felt like a party inside the plaza. But outside, thousands of anti-gay Christian protesters demonstrated against the pride celebration, chanting slogans and blasting Korean-language gospel music.

"You have the rather angry protesters, broadcasting their music across here, trying to compete with the party atmosphere on the inside," says Phillip Kendall, the political secretary at the British Embassy in Seoul, which supports the pride festival with a booth every year.

Kendall says it will take time for Korean society overall to celebrate diversity.

"They still have a conservative view in this country to what life should be and what society should be," he says.

There have been some gains for members of the LGBT community in East Asia—Taiwan recently OK'ed same-sex marriage, for example.

But South Korea still criminalizes it. And this spring, for the first time, the military enforced a longstanding ban on homosexual activity and sentenced a gay soldier to six months in jail for having consensual sex with another soldier in a private place. Amnesty International called this part of "an outrageous military gay witch-hunt."

Donghuan Kim, a volunteer with a nonprofit called Military Human Rights Korea that's working to try and change the law, says he was "horrified" by the gay soldier's sentencing. "Younger generations are very open-minded and trying to accept homosexual community to the major society," he says. "But there are 10 million Christians out there. They're very, very homophobic."

His estimate of South Korea's Christian population is actually low, as it has grown over the years. Nearly a third of all 50 million Koreans identify as Christian, and they make up a powerful lobby for traditional values.

Pastor Joseph Joo heads an organization in Seoul called Anti-Homosexuality Christian Solidarity, a group of a few hundred churchgoers who start social media campaigns supporting unions of one man and one woman. South Korea isn't ready to accept sexual minorities, Joo insists.

"Christians make up a huge part of South Korea's public life and they have taken a big role in Korea's modernization. We feel that because homosexuality goes against biblical teachings, it's emotionally unacceptable to the public," he says.

He also cites South Korea's birth rate—the lowest among the world's richest nations—as a reason why he's against same-sex couples.

"As a result of homosexuality, there is no birth," he says. "And relationships are distorted and destroyed."

> **South Korea's institutions and political class are only reluctantly tolerating sexual minorities.**

South Korea's new president, Moon Jae-in, hails from a progressive party. But when he was pressed during the campaign, he, too, said he opposed homosexuality.

After an outcry, Moon, who is Catholic, apologized—kind of. He said he shouldn't have been judgmental.

Kendall, the British diplomat, says foreign advocates of LGBT rights shouldn't be judgmental, either. "All of our countries went through this years ago," he says. "So we cannot have a holier-than-thou attitude when it comes to these issues. But we try to explain how we got over the issues which Korea is experiencing today."

He and other LGBT rights supporters in South Korea say certain things are making a difference: a pride festival that grows bigger every year, rising international pressure on Korea from the diplomatic community in Seoul and regional neighbors making progress. Parts of Tokyo, like Taiwan, have OK'ed same-sex unions.

"In comparison to other [pride celebrations] in the world, there's more protest out here, as you can see. But it makes me want to fight against them and it makes me want to win," says Lee, the actor.

He and his troupe are dressed in their faux-silk bathrobes for a reason. Later in the day, they all shed those robes during a performance—an artistic expression of coming out. In a country where homosexuality is considered taboo, their radical act is simply being themselves.

Print Citations

CMS: Hu, Elise. "For South Korea's LGBT Community, an Uphill Battle for Rights." In *The Reference Shelf: The Two Koreas*, edited by Micah L. Issit, 36-38. Ipswich, MA: H.W. Wilson, 2019.

MLA: Hu, Elise. "For South Korea's LGBT Community, an Uphill Battle for Rights." *The Reference Shelf: The Two Koreas,* edited by Micah L. Issit, H.W. Wilson, 2019, pp. 36-38.

APA: Hu, E. (2019). For South Korea's LGBT community, an uphill battle for rights. In Micah L. Issit (Ed.), *The reference shelf: The two Koreas* (pp. 36-38). Ipswich, MA: H.W. Wilson.

What Is Life Like in North Korea?

The Week, June 11, 2018

As Donald Trump meets with North Korean leader Kim Jong Un in Singapore this week, many hope the US president will raise the issue of human rights.

Asked by a reporter over the weekend whether he would voice concerns about North Korea's gulags, or prison camps, "Trump said all issues would come up at the summit," reports *CBS News*.

Daily life in North Korea has come under greater scrutiny over the past few years as worries about political stability in the region have intensified.

If you "merged the Soviet Union under Stalin with an ancient Chinese Empire, mixed in *The Truman Show* and then made the whole thing Holocaust-esque, you have modern-day North Korea," says *HuffPost's* Tim Urban.

"It's a dictatorship of the most extreme kind, a cult of personality beyond anything Stalin or Mao could have imagined," Urban continues, adding that the secretive country keeps "both the outside world and its own people completely in the dark about one another—a true hermit kingdom."

So what is life like in North Korea?

A Truly Depressive State

Human Rights Watch describes North Korea as "one of the most repressive authoritarian states in the world."

According to the influential NGO, the regime "curtails all basic human rights, including freedom of expression, assembly, and association, and freedom to practice religion. It prohibits any organised political opposition, independent media, free trade unions, and independent civil society organisations. Arbitrary arrest, torture in custody, forced labour, and public executions maintain an environment of fear and control."

A 2017 report by the International Bar Association (IBA) estimated that the North is holding between 80,000 and 130,000 political prisoners, who suffer intense persecution.

According to the report, these abuses include "systematic murder (including infanticide), torture, persecution of Christians, rape, forced abortions, starvation and overwork leading to countless deaths.

The IBA describes specific incidents of prisoners tortured and killed for their religious affiliation, with North Korean officials told "to wipe out the seed of [Christian] reactionaries."

Daily Struggle

All North Koreans need permission to live in the capital Pyongyang (there are roadblocks on the city's streets to prevent unauthorised travel). Most of Pyongyang's inhabitants are supports of the ruling Workers' Party of Korea (WPK), who have a higher position in society.

Much of the city operates an "alternative suspension of electricity supply" system, meaning that when buildings on one side of the street are blacked out, the other side of the street gets power. When the switchover time arrives, "there is a mad rush of children as they head for their friends' apartments across the road," says Paul French author of *North Korea: State of Paranoia.*

"The scarcity of cars, the early nights, the absence of entertainment venues, and the electricity shortages, mean that by midnight Pyongyang is effectively a ghost city, and remains so until 6am the next day," he continues.

Food shopping is equally problematic. "Staples such as soy sauce, soybean paste, salt and oil, as well as toothpaste, soap, underwear and shoes, sell out fast," says French.

The range of food items available is highly restricted. The main staple of the North Korean diet is rice, "though bread is sometimes available, accompanied by a form of butter that is often rancid," he adds.

Outside the capital, "any buildings of grandeur quickly disappear, save for the large bronze statues of the Eternal President Kim Il Sung," grandfather of Kim Jong Un, says travel blog *Time Travel Turtle.* Green fields of corn and rice stretch from the road to the mountains on the horizon, "but this belies the poverty and rustic lifestyles of the citizens," notes the site.

> **Human Rights Watch describes North Korea as "one of the most repressive authoritarian states in the world."**

Enforced Celebrations

The Mass Games takes place four days a week for three months every summer. It involves 100,000 performers, many of them young children, "depicting the glorious history and thriving modernity of North Korea," says *HuffPost's* Urban. "The backdrop is a stunning tapestry made of 20,000 kids holding up large coloured cards."

The Games perfectly sum up North Korea, he adds, as an event that is "centered on propaganda, stresses the collective over the individual, and makes no sense as a priority given the state of things."

A Reason to Leave

The number of successful defectors peaked in 2009, when 2,914 North Koreans arrived in South Korea, but since then the number has more than halved. Only 1,418 made it across in 2016, according to latest figures from South Korea's Unification Ministry, which predicts an even smaller figure for the following year.

"Increased border controls by both North Korea and China are thought to be the primary reason for the drop," CNN reports.

But increasingly, North Koreans "are not fleeing their totalitarian state because they are hungry, as they did during the 15 or so years following the outbreak of a devastating famine in the mid-1990s. Now, they are leaving because they are disillusioned," says the *Washington Post*.

"Market activity is exploding, and with that comes a flow of information, whether as chit-chat from traders who cross into China or as soap operas loaded on USB sticks," the newspaper explains. "And this leads many North Koreans to dream in a way they hadn't before."

Print Citations

CMS: "What Is Life Like in North Korea?" In *The Reference Shelf: The Two Koreas*, edited by Micah L. Issit, 39-41. Ipswich, MA: H.W. Wilson, 2019.

MLA: "What Is Life Like in North Korea?" *The Reference Shelf: The Two Koreas,* edited by Micah L. Issit, H.W. Wilson, 2019, pp. 39-41.

APA: The Week. (2019). What is life like in North Korea? In Micah L. Issit (Ed.), *The reference shelf: The two Koreas* (pp. 39-41). Ipswich, MA: H.W. Wilson.

What Life Is Like for Ordinary North Koreans

The Economist, May 26, 2018

They have vanishingly few opportunities to speak to foreigners and, even when they are allowed to, risk landing in a labour camp if caught saying the wrong thing. Yet North Koreans are full of curiosity about the outside world. On a recent visit, your correspondent was asked about the place of civil servants in capitalist society, about how Western manufacturers keep costs down and, inevitably, about Brexit. Any information about foreigners is highly prized. "We want to know how you think," said one inquisitive local, "so that when things change, we're ready."

"Things changing" has seemed like a tantalising possibility ever since Kim Jong Un, the North's leader, embarked on a diplomatic charm offensive earlier this year. In Pyongyang, where most people can access accounts of the rapprochement with America and South Korea in the state media, some are allowing themselves to dream. One woman said she wanted to go to Britain and South-East Asia. Another asked your correspondent to help her practise her French because she hoped to travel to Paris if the diplomatic efforts paid off.

Yet hopes that Mr Kim will bring change, which were widespread when he took over from his father in 2011, have so far proved misplaced. Far from liberalising the country, Mr Kim has tightened the shackles, reinforcing the border with China to make it harder for people to escape and cracking down hard on offences such as possessing a flash drive loaded with South Korean soap operas, or owning a Chinese SIM card in order to make international calls near the border. (Ordinary citizens are not allowed to call foreigners within the country, much less anyone abroad.)

Pyongyang welcomes visitors with a relentless onslaught of murals, monuments and portraits of Mr Kim and his father and grandfather, who ran the country before him. Primary-school children decked out in traditional costumes sing songs about their glory. "Let us accomplish the programmatic task our dearest supreme leader Kim Jong Un proposed in his New Year address" runs one catchy slogan. Drivers have to slow down when they pass enormous bronze statues of the dead deities. Out-of-towners are compelled to wash their cars before crossing the city limits, lest they mar the capital's aesthetic.

That aesthetic involves pastel-coloured apartment blocks, pretty flower-shaped streetlights and pleasant parks kept impeccably clean by residents. Work crews of middle-aged women dressed in bright orange can be seen at all hours planting flowers and ripping out weeds on the grassy verges around town. To those who can pay, the city affords a measure of material comfort, despite the recent tightening of sanctions. Restau-

> **Only those deemed loyal to the regime are allowed to live in the capital. Life outside is far worse.**

rants offer pizza, pasta and sushi as well as semi-Western entertainment. At one restaurant the staff band performs stirring renditions of "Arirang," a traditional Korean tune, and "Can you feel the love tonight?," a schmaltzy duet from a Disney movie. Petrol and diesel prices have fallen by almost 20% after a spike in April, suggesting that China has relaxed its enforcement of the international sanctions that restrict North Korea's oil imports.

Yet there are signs that even the showcase capital is struggling. Long-term foreign residents note that fancier restaurants and coffee shops look less busy than they did. (By contrast, grimy city-centre bars serving beer and cheap spirits are crammed even on weekday evenings.) Buses and trams, though gleaming, operate several times over capacity, with people hanging out of the windows and enormous queues at stops. In many buildings the lifts are mostly out of service and corridors remain dark, hinting at a less-than-perfect electricity supply (though some of the capital's well-to-do get around the problem by installing solar panels on their balconies).

North Koreans are compelled to spend six days a week working for the state for meagre wages. Most get little choice in what they do, causing well-qualified people to complain of mind-numbing work with no prospects. "My job is just a dull waste of time," says one woman in her 20s who works for a state-run firm. Asked about quitting, she demurs: "It's not easy."

Patriotic Brick-Laying

Young men have to spend years doing military service, which mostly amounts to hard labour on construction sites. Many young women work in factories far from home, where they live crammed into spartan dormitories. The only day off—Sunday—features group discussions about how output can be improved.

The workers in factories on the outskirts of Pyongyang are also permitted to visit the city on Sundays, in the hope of finding a local husband. (North Korean women are encouraged to marry young, often to a husband selected by their family, and are derided as "rotten fish" if they remain single in their late 20s.) But on the whole, personal life is restricted. Beyond contact with one's family and colleagues, socialising is discouraged.

Only those deemed loyal to the regime are allowed to live in the capital. Life outside is far worse. The WHO says that 40% of the population is malnourished. Electricity and proper plumbing are rarities. Unlike in Pyongyang, people have fewer ways of getting around sanctions, which are starting to cause shortages of fuel and fertiliser, according to NGOs that work in the country. Agricultural technology remains primitive. Visiting experts say they still encounter farming equipment from the 1950s. Just beyond the city limits of Pyongyang, farmers are still ploughing fields with oxen; women carry big bundles of firewood on their backs. On the hills, anti-aircraft guns tower over the squat one-storey villages. News of the outside world comes mainly in the form of a weekly briefing from a party official.

And even in Pyongyang, Western and South Korean pressure groups attest, the deadening totalitarian system is as intrusive as ever. People are encouraged to keep an eye on the political reliability of friends, family and co-workers, and are rewarded for reporting misdeeds. Even minor infringements, such as perusing smuggled religious pamphlets, can result in severe punishment. Unguarded remarks about the leader or one of his predecessors may lead to banishment from Pyongyang or, in more egregious cases, being carted off to a prison camp—sometimes with one's family in tow. The UN estimated in 2014 that between 80,000 and 120,000 people were held in such camps, where torture, indiscriminate beatings and starvation are commonplace. The number seems to have stayed roughly constant since then. No wonder North Koreans are curious about different ways of doing things.

Print Citations

CMS: "What Life Is Like for Ordinary North Koreans." In *The Reference Shelf: The Two Koreas*, edited by Micah L. Issit, 42-44. Ipswich, MA: H.W. Wilson, 2019.

MLA: "What Life Is Like for Ordinary North Koreans." *The Reference Shelf: The Two Koreas*, edited by Micah L. Issit, H.W. Wilson, 2019, pp. 42-44.

APA: The Economist. (2019). What life is like for ordinary North Koreans. In Micah L. Issit (Ed.), *The reference shelf: The two Koreas* (pp. 42-44). Ipswich, MA: H.W. Wilson.

3
The Korean Threat

By Stefan Krasowski, via Wikimedia.

A North Korean ballistic missile on display on North Korea Victory Day, 2013. North Korea's most recent missiles are capable of reaching the continental United States, but warhead re-entry and accuracy technology remains unproven.

Widoghan (Dangerous) Days

How one views the North Korea nuclear controversy relates to the threat one perceives from an armed North Korean state. Some believe that North Korea poses a direct military threat and have speculated that North Korean dictator Kim Jong-Un is unstable enough to use nuclear weapons against the United States despite the fact that such an act would mean the end of North Korean civilization. For others, the entire saga of North Korea's nuclear weapons program is part of an elaborate effort to defend against potential regime change or to strengthen the nation's bargaining position within the international community.

History of Nuclear Negotiations

Duyeon Kim, senior fellow at the Seoul-based Korean Peninsula Future Forum, explained in an interview with *Frontline* that North Korea's nuclear weapons program began during the Korean War when the country feared that the United States might use a nuclear weapon against Korea as it had to attack Japan during World War II. "Ever since the Korean War, they always assumed that Washington would attack them any day and wipe them out. The only way for them to survive and not get attacked would be to develop the most powerful weapon on Earth, which would be the nuclear bomb."[1]

Though this threat was never made explicit, declassified documents make it clear that President Dwight Eisenhower's administration was actively considering using atomic weapons against both North Korea and China in 1953, in order to break the deadlock in the war.[2] Though this atomic strike never came to pass, the leaked documents revealed detailed plans and strategies, validating the threat perceived by North Korea at the time.

In the 1960s, as the nuclear arsenals of the former Soviet Union and the United States continued to develop, it was realized that both nations had reached a stage of "mutually assured destruction." The United States, Russia, and other global leaders then began to negotiate toward nuclear non-proliferation—preventing new nations from developing nuclear arsenals and nations already in possession of nuclear weapons from developing more of them. This effort to end the nuclear arms race resulted in the 1968 International Nuclear Non-Proliferation Treaty (NPT), an agreement between the United States, Russia, the UK, and a number of other countries. As of 2018, 190 states have submitted to the agreement, which includes three pillars: disarmament, nonproliferation, and peaceful use of nuclear energy. The treaty further specifies a UN-designated system of inspection wherein signatory nations are bound to submit to inspection, if deemed necessary by the UN.[3]

After the Korean War, the United States and allied attitudes toward North Korea remained hostile, and the United States maintained serious economic sanctions that limited North Korea's capability for international trade. Given the widespread poverty and lack of resources in North Korea even before the war, international sanctions deepened the nation's material challenges and poverty. With financial and material aid from the former Soviet Union, North Korea began work on its first nuclear complex after the war and completed work on its first nuclear reactor, Yongbyon, in the early 1980s. Though news of North Korea's nuclear program was controversial, the government in Pyongyang insisted that its nuclear program was peaceful and intended only to meet the nation's very real energy demands. In 1985, North Korea agreed to sign on to the NPT and also signed a 1991 agreement with South Korea, with both countries agreeing not to pursue nuclear weapon technology. However, North Korea subsequently refused to submit to international inspections, reigniting the controversy in the early 1990s.[4]

In 2002, the Bush administration accused North Korea of operating a secret weapons program and the following year North Korea withdrew from the NPT. That same year, intelligence reports indicated that North Korea had reactivated the Yongbyon facility. North Korea announced, in April of 2003, that the country already had nuclear weapons. In July of 2006, North Korea tested long-range missiles, resulting in condemnation from the UN. In October of that year, the DPRK claimed to have tested a functional nuclear weapon. After another series of failed negotiation attempts, North Korea announced the completion of a second nuclear test in May of 2009.[5] This development was followed by another series of talks, with little progress, followed by a third nuclear test carried out in February of 2013, sparking yet another round of sanctions and criticism from the international community.[6]

In 2015, North Korea claimed to have the ability to construct nuclear missiles and later announced that the country had successfully manufactured a hydrogen bomb. In 2016, they claimed to have successfully tested a nuclear missile. In 2017, North Korea tested their first intercontinental ballistic missile (ICBM) and then issued a threat that the nation would be prepared to strike the United States if the US government attempted to remove Kim Jong-Un from power. Another nuclear test came in September of that year, amid rising tensions between the United States and North Korea. This began a battle of insults between the leaders of the two countries, followed by announcements of an unprecedented summit between Kim and President Donald Trump, and a temporary cessation of nuclear testing in 2018.

The Best Defense

What is clear from statements made by the Kim family and through North Korea's Korean Central News Agency (KCNA) is that the North Korean nuclear program has been motivated by the Kim family's nearly 70-year concern that the United States seeks to remove them from power. While it is unclear if any administration, past or present, has realistically considered warfare with North Korea in order to end the Kim regime, there are many in the United States and around the world who would welcome such a change. Further, numerous past US presidents have openly criticized the Kim regime. George W. Bush and Donald Trump have accused the

DPRK of supporting terrorism and both issued direct military threats against the Kim regime.

As of 2019, American political analysts are divided as to whether or not North Korea poses a credible nuclear threat to the United States. The United States, on the other hand, possesses the capability to eliminate North Korea's military and governmental institutions as well as its population. Any scenario involving warfare between the two nations, no matter which nation strikes first, would be disastrous for both and for the world in general. The United States cannot directly strike North Korea without risking the lives of the more than 30,000 US troops located in South Korea and the more than 5 million citizens of South Korea. Hundreds of thousands living in China, Japan, and Russia would also be put at risk. Also, Northeast Asia is among the most strategic economic regions in the world and so any warfare with North Korea, nuclear or otherwise, would likely initiate severe economic turmoil.[7]

Beyond Convention

National security analysts and experts have long warned that direct military threat is not the most plausible or likely danger posed by North Korea. Rather, it is through the black market and emerging modes of unconventional warfare that North Korea poses its most potent and realistic threat to global security.

North Korea has a long history of weapons dealing to dictatorial regimes and can sell weapons, designs, technological components, or nuclear material to other nations or rogue states. Since the 1960s, when North Koreawas provided with military support through the former Soviet Union, they have funneled weapons into like-minded regimes in other parts of the world. The concern is that North Korea could raise the global threat of nuclear conflict, even if this conflict does not occur in Northeast Asia.[8]

Intelligence reports indicate that, despite UN and other governmental sanctions and widespread poverty, North Korea has used nonstate actors and proxies to conduct numerous weapons deals with other nations and rogue states. North Korea and Syria have had a military-trade relationship since the 1960s when both nations were under Russian influence and it is believed that this relationship has continued, with North Korea supporting the current Syrian regime of dictatorial leader Bashar al-Assad. More recently, press reports indicated that North Korea sold the Syrian military the chemical weapons that were used against Syrian anti-Assad rebels in 2017. It is also believed that North Korea has sent troops and technical advisors to Syria to assist in the development of the Syrian military. Beginning in the 1980s, North Korea became a supplier of missiles and rockets to the Lebanese organization Hezbollah, and CIA data suggests further arms deals to Iran and Iraqi forces, prior to the US invasion of Iraq.[9]

Further, though North Korea's technological capacity is far less advanced than that of the United States and other developed nations, some national security analysts believe that North Korea poses a cyberwarfare threat to the United States. Dmitry Alperovitch, head of the information security firm Crowdstrike that investigated the 2016 Russian hack of the Democratic National Committee, told the *Guardian* in February of 2018:

> In 2018, my biggest worry is actually about North Korea. I worry a great deal that they may do a destructive attack, perhaps against our financial sector, in an attempt to deter a potential US strike against either their nuclear facilities or even the regime itself. Regardless of whether a military strike is actually in the cards or not, what matters is whether they think one might happen. And given all the rhetoric over the last year or so, it wouldn't be irrational for them to assume that.[10]

North Korea's cyberwarfare capability became clear in 2017 when North Korean state-sponsored hackers were connected to the release of the "WannaCry" ransomware program that disrupted digital systems at Britain's National Health Service and Spanish telecom company Telefónica, as well as other systems in the Ukraine, Russia, and Taiwan. Ransomware is a type of program capable of identifying, isolating, and freezing data on a computer system. Typically, the operator of the ransomware contacts the system administrator demanding a ransom for the release of the seized data. In the case of the WannaCry attack, which affected nearly 230,000 computers in 150 countries, the operators of the malware requested $300 per computer to cease their attack. The North Korean hacker program was found to have exploited vulnerabilities in Windows-based systems revealed through leaked NSA documents. Though US intelligence implicated North Korean hackers as early as June, it wasn't until December of 2017 that the US government, in conjunction with the UK and other European Union members, officially released a statement accusing North Korea of launching the attack.[11]

Given that North Korea has demonstrated the capability of launching a cyberattack with global reach, many national security experts believe that the nation already possesses sufficient technological expertise to potentially launch more impactful attacks against the United States. Because such attacks are difficult to trace, a skillfully deployed cyberattack may occur before the target company, governmental agency, or individual can identify and respond. Though data on US cyberwarfare is limited, it is known that the United States has developed and used cyberweapons on potential enemy states in the past, outside of formal declarations of hostilities. It is believed, for instance, that a secret government-led cyberattack orchestrated by the Obama administration resulted in the failure of a North Korean missile test in 2017 when the test missiles veered uncontrollably off course and into the sea.[12] While the US government never admitted culpability, it has been established that the United States has the capability to directly disrupt digitally controlled weapons systems in other nations. The potential for a future North Korean cyberthreat, as well as the intensification of North Korea's nuclear weapons program, is believed to have instigated new US investment and development of cyberweaponry to counter potential threats.

Options and Alternatives

Whether or not future warfare with North Korea is likely to occur, North Korea poses a serious challenge to the United States in terms of economic development, foreign relations, and national security. North Korea is a society marginalized by widespread poverty and limited resources and controlled by an increasingly fragile military regime. Internal dissidence may bring about the end of the Kim dynasty. Given the high potential cost of war, the United States and allies in the international community have no better option than negotiation and diplomacy.

Works Used

Bechtol, Bruce E. Jr. "North Korea's Illegal Weapons Trade." *Foreign Affairs*. Jun 6, 2018. Retrieved from https://www.foreignaffairs.com/articles/north-korea/2018-06-06/north-koreas-illegal-weapons-trade.

Boghani, Priyanka. "The U.S. and North Korea on the Brink: A Timeline." *Frontline*. PBS. Apr 18, 2018. Retrieved from https://www.pbs.org/wgbh/frontline/article/the-u-s-and-north-korea-on-the-brink-a-timeline/.

Gwertzman, Bernard. "U.S. Papers Tell of '53 Policy to Use A-Bomb in Korea." *The New York Times*. The New York Times Co. Jun 8, 1984. Retrieved from https://www.nytimes.com/1984/06/08/world/us-papers-tell-of-53-policy-to-use-a-bomb-in-korea.html.

Hern, Alex. "North Korea Is a Bigger Cyber-Attack Threat Than Russia, Says Expert." *The Guardian*. The Guardian News and Media. Feb 26, 2018. Retrieved from https://www.theguardian.com/technology/2018/feb/26/north-korea-cyber-attack-threat-russia.

Nakashima, Ellen and Philip Rucker. "U.S. Declares North Korea Carried Out Massive WannaCry Cyberattack." *The Washington Post*. The Washington Post Co. Dec 19, 2017. Retrieved from https://www.washingtonpost.com/world/national-security/us-set-to-declare-north-korea-carried-out-massive-wannacry-cyber-attack/2017/12/18/509deb1c-e446-11e7-a65d-1ac0fd7f097e_story.html?noredirect=on&utm_term=.e36f96a97ba3.

"North Korea Nuclear Timeline Fast Facts." *CNN*. CNN. Apr 3, 2018. Retrieved from https://www.cnn.com/2013/10/29/world/asia/north-korea-nuclear-timeline---fast-facts/index.html.

Payne, Ed. "World Leaders React to North Korea's Nuclear Test." *CNN*. CNN. Feb 12, 2013. Retrieved from https://www.cnn.com/2013/02/12/world/north-korea-nuclear-reax/.

Pollack, Jonathan D. "The Threat from North Korea." *Brookings*. Brookings Institution. Apr 24, 2017. Retrieved from https://www.brookings.edu/blog/unpacked/2017/04/24/the-threat-from-north-korea/.

Ramani, Samuel. "North Korea's Syrian Connection." *The Diplomat*. Feb 27, 2018. Retrieved from https://thediplomat.com/2018/02/north-koreas-syrian-connection/.

Sanger, David E. and William J. Broad. "Trump Inherits a Secret Cyberwar Against North Korean Missiles." *The New York Times*. Mar 4, 2017. Retrieved from https://www.nytimes.com/2017/03/04/world/asia/north-korea-missile-program-sabotage.html?module=inline.

"Treaty on the Non-Proliferation of Nuclear Weapons (NPT)." *UN*. United Nations Office for Disarmament Affairs. Retrieved from https://www.un.org/disarmament/wmd/nuclear/npt/.

"World Outraged by North Korea's Latest Nuke Threat." *CNN*. CNN. May 25, 2009. Retrieved from http://www.cnn.com/2009/WORLD/asiapcf/05/24/nkorea.nuclear/index.html?section=cnn_latest.

Notes

1. Boghani, "The U.S. and North Korea on the Brink: A Timeline."
2. Gwetzman, "U.S. Papers Tell of '53 Policy to Use A-Bomb in Korea."
3. "Treaty on the Non-Proliferation of Nuclear Weapons (NPT)," *UN*.
4. "North Korea Nuclear Timeline Fast Facts," *CNN*.
5. "World outraged by North Korea's Latest Nuke Test," *CNN*.
6. Payne, "World Leaders React to North Korea's Nuclear Test."
7. Pollack, "The Threat from North Korea."
8. Bechtol, "North Korea's Illegal Weapons Trade."
9. Ramani, "North Korea's Syrian Connection."
10. 1Hern, "North Korea Is a Bigger Cyber-Attack Than Russia, Says Expert."
11. 1Nakashima and Rucker, "U.S. Declares North Korea Carried Out Massive WannaCry Cyberattack."
12. Sanger and Broad, "Trump Inherits a Secret Cyberwar Against North Korean Missiles."

How the Nuclear-Armed Nations Brought the North Korea Crisis on Themselves

By Simon Tisdall

The Guardian, September 5, 2017

North Korea's defiant pursuit of nuclear weapons capabilities, dramatised by last weekend's powerful underground test and a recent long-range ballistic missile launch over Japan, has been almost universally condemned as posing a grave, unilateral threat to international peace and security.

The growing North Korean menace also reflects the chronic failure of multilateral counter-proliferation efforts and, in particular, the longstanding refusal of acknowledged nuclear-armed states such as the US and Britain to honour a legal commitment to reduce and eventually eliminate their arsenals.

In other words, the past and present leaders of the US, Russia, China, France and the UK, whose governments signed but have not fulfilled the terms of the 1970 nuclear non-proliferation treaty (NPT), have to some degree brought the North Korea crisis on themselves. Kim Jong-un's recklessness and bad faith is a product of their own.

The NPT, signed by 191 countries, is probably the most successful arms control treaty ever. When conceived in 1968, at the height of the cold war, the mass proliferation of nuclear weapons was considered a real possibility. Since its inception and prior to North Korea, only India, Pakistan and Israel are known to have joined the nuclear "club" in almost half a century.

To work fully, the NPT relies on keeping a crucial bargain: non-nuclear-armed states agree never to acquire the weapons, while nuclear-armed states agree to share the benefits of peaceful nuclear technology and pursue nuclear disarmament with the ultimate aim of eliminating them. This, in effect, was the guarantee offered to vulnerable, insecure outlier states such as North Korea. The guarantee was a dud, however, and the bargain has never been truly honoured.

Rather than reducing their nuclear arsenals, the US, Russia and China have modernised and expanded them. Britain has eliminated some of its capability, but it is nevertheless renewing and updating Trident. France clings fiercely to its *"force de frappe."* Altogether, the main nuclear-weapon states have an estimated 22,000 nuclear bombs. A report by the non-governmental British-American Security Information Council in May said nuclear security was getting worse.

Multilateral forums for advancing nuclear disarmament are in crisis.

"The need for nuclear disarmament through multilateral diplomacy is greater now than it has been at any stage since the end of the cold war. Trust and confidence in the existing nuclear non-proliferation regime is fraying, tensions are high, goals are misaligned and dialogue is irregular," the report said.

"Internationally, relationships between the nuclear-weapon states have deteriorated, in particular between the US and Russia, and to some extent, China … All nuclear-armed states are modernising their nuclear forces, at a worldwide cost of $1tn per decade … Attention tends to be focused on specific cases of proliferation concern, such as North Korea and Iran, at the expense of the bigger picture."

Multilateral forums for advancing nuclear disarmament are in crisis. The next NPT review conference is not due until 2020. Like its 2015 predecessor, it is not expected to achieve much. The UN-backed conference on disarmament, which helped produce conventions banning biological and chemical weapons and initiated the 1996 comprehensive test ban treaty, is politically polarised and struggling to agree key measures such as a fissile material cut-off treaty.

Meanwhile, as South Korea and Japan consider acquiring nuclear weapons, Donald Trump appears irrationally determined to scrap one of the few recent arms control successes—the landmark 2015 nuclear deal with Iran.

There has been one big breakthrough this year, the under-reported adoption by 122 countries at the UN in July of a new treaty on the prohibition of nuclear weapons, which envisages an outright ban on the use of all nukes. It has, however, been potentially fatally undermined by a boycott by the nuclear powers. The US, Britain and France declared, cynically as critics saw it, that they preferred to stick with the never-ending NPT route to disarmament. "This initiative clearly disregards the realities of the international security environment," they said in a joint statement.

The ineffectiveness of current arms control and counter-proliferation efforts has helped to create an environment in which North Korea, allegedly using smuggled, Russian-designed ballistic missile engines, is rapidly advancing its nuclear ambitions with apparent impunity, at great risk to international stability.

Multilateral arms control failures also mean the Korean "solution" Trump talks about with increasing frequency—the use of preventive military action, notwithstanding its illegality under international law—could, if applied, spell the end of deterrence and the beginning of an unchecked global nuclear arms race.

Print Citations

CMS: Tisdall, Simon. "How the Nuclear-Armed Nations Brought the North Korea Crisis on Themselves." In *The Reference Shelf: The Two Koreas*, edited by Micah L. Issit, 53-55. Ipswich, MA: H.W. Wilson, 2019.

MLA: Tisdall, Simon. "How the Nuclear-Armed Nations Brought the North Korea Crisis on Themselves." *The Reference Shelf: The Two Koreas,* edited by Micah L. Issit, H.W. Wilson, 2019, pp. 53-55.

APA: Tisdall, S. (2019). How the nuclear-armed nations brought the North Korea crisis on themselves. In Micah L. Issit (Ed.), *The reference shelf: The two Koreas* (pp. 53-55). Ipswich, MA: H.W. Wilson.

How North Korea's Hackers Became Dangerously Good

By Timothy W. Martin
The Wall Street Journal, April 19, 2018

SEOUL—North Korea's cyber army, long considered a midlevel security threat, is quietly morphing into one of the world's most sophisticated and dangerous hacking machines.

Over the past 18 months, the nation's fingerprints have appeared in an increasing number of cyberattacks, the skill level of its hackers has rapidly improved and their targets have become more worrisome, a *Wall Street Journal* examination of the program reveals. As recently as March, suspected North Korean hackers appear to have infiltrated Turkish banks and invaded computer systems in the run-up to the Winter Olympics, cybersecurity researchers say.

For years, cybersecurity experts viewed North Korea as a second-rate hacking force whose attacks were disruptive but reasonably easy to decode. Researchers rated its operational skills well behind countries such as Russia, Israel and the U.S.

Those days appear to be over, with Pyongyang flashing levels of originality in its coding and techniques that have surprised researchers. It also has shown a willingness to go after targets such as central banks and point-of-sale systems. As North Korea prepares for possible negotiations with Washington aimed at freezing its nuclear program, its hacking capabilities could help it generate money to compensate for economic sanctions or to threaten foreign financial institutions.

North Korea is cultivating elite hackers much like other countries train Olympic athletes, according to defectors and South Korean cyber and intelligence experts. Promising students are identified as young as 11 years old and funneled into special schools, where they are taught hacking and how to develop computer viruses.

"Once you have been selected to get into the cyber unit, you receive a title that makes you a special citizen, and you don't have to worry about food and the basic necessities," says a defector familiar with North Korea's cyber training.

To assess North Korea's cyber program, the *Journal* interviewed dozens of North Korean defectors, foreign cybersecurity researchers, South Korean government advisers and military experts. The researchers emphasize that catching hackers is difficult, and that they can't be 100% certain that every attack attributed to North Korea was orchestrated by its cyberwarriors.

These experts point to numerous signs that the hackers have become better. North Koreans are acting on security glitches in widely used software only days after the vulnerabilities first appear, and crafting malicious code so advanced it isn't detected by antivirus programs, they say. When software or security firms plug holes, the hackers are adapting within days or weeks, fine-tuning their malware much as Apple Inc. would release an update to the iPhone's operating system.

Many North Korean hackers are using perfect English or embedding other languages into coding to make it appear hacks came from other countries, the researchers have concluded. And they are earning a reputation as innovators at breaking into smartphones, hiding malware in Bible apps or using Facebook Inc. to help infect targets.

"The whole world needs to take notice," says John Hultquist, director of intelligence analysis at U.S. cybersecurity firm FireEye Inc., who now ranks North Korea among the world's mature hacking operations.

North Korea has denied involvement in hacking attacks, including last year's WannaCry ransomware, which locked digital files and demanded bitcoin payment for their release, or the 2016 cybertheft of $81 million from Bangladesh's central bank. Calls for comment to the North Korean consulate in Hong Kong weren't answered.

Researchers say telltale signs are buried deep inside the malware and coding: Korean words only used in the North, the use of data servers commonly associated with Pyongyang hacks and files created by usernames linked with the country's hackers.

The U.S. and other governments have publicly blamed North Korea for an array of infiltrations in recent months, including WannaCry, citing patterns in coding and techniques they say lead to Pyongyang. South Korean officials estimate their country is now targeted by an estimated 1.5 million North Korean hacking attempts daily, or 17 every second.

Growing Threat

Attacks that cyber experts suspect were orchestrated by North Korea are becoming more frequent.

- December 2014: Emails are stolen in attack on Sony Pictures Entertainment.

- February 2016: $81 million is stolen from Bangladesh central bank.

- May 2017: WannaCry ransomware attack infects more than 300,000 computers in 150 countries.

- November 2017: Adobe Flash "zero-day" malware is embedded in Microsoft Office files in South Korea.

- December 2017: South Korea cryptocurrency exchange Youbit is hacked, causing company to declare bankruptcy.

- December 2017: Attacks on South Korean groups affiliated with the Winter Olympics.

- January 2018: Tokyo-based Coincheck cryptocurrency exchange says about $530 million was stolen.
- March 2018: Adobe Flash "zero-day" attack on Turkish financial institutions and government groups.

Late last year, North Korean hackers were the first to unearth a vulnerability in the popular Adobe Flash multimedia player that allowed an unchallenged attack to go undetected for months, according to cybersecurity researchers. After Adobe released a security patch in February, the suspected Pyongyang cyberwarriors modified the malware to target European financial institutions, giving them the ability to steal sensitive information about their networks, according to cybersecurity firm McAfee LLC.

North Korea's cyber advances parallel its breakthroughs in missile technology since Kim Jong Un assumed power in 2011.

Many suspected North Korean attacks occur without a clear objective. Some researchers have described it as akin to an organized-crime ring seeking any weaknesses to learn about enemies or generate cash. Researchers generally agree the program is becoming more focused on obtaining military intelligence or earning income as sanctions tighten and negotiations with the U.S. approach.

"Hacking abilities give them a much stronger hand at the negotiating table," says Ross Rustici, a director at cybersecurity firm Cybereason Inc. and a former Defense Department analyst.

In October, South Korean lawmakers said North Koreans had stolen 235 gigabytes of data and military secrets, including a joint U.S.-South Korean plan to eliminate Pyongyang leadership in the event of war. North Korean hackers are believed to have stolen hundreds of millions of dollars, ranging from stealing credit-card information from ATMs to a $530 million raid of a Japanese cryptocurrency exchange in January.

Cryptocurrencies appear to be a particular interest. Last year, suspected North Korean hackers began creating fictitious Facebook profiles, posing as attractive young women interested in bitcoin or working in the industry, according to people familiar with a South Korean investigation into the matter. They sought friendships with men at cryptocurrency exchanges and banks.

The Facebook accounts listed links with an "NYU Research Center" and other institutions to make them appear believable. Then the hackers lured men into opening app downloads or Microsoft Word documents, disguised as greeting cards or invites, that flooded their systems with malware, say the people familiar with the investigation.

It isn't clear what the scheme netted. Facebook shut down fake accounts used by hackers linked to North Korea that "pretended to be other people in order to do things like learning about others and building relationships with potential targets," the company said in December.

North Korea also has been using a targeting "watering hole" attack, in which a person's computer becomes infected by accessing a certain website, according to cybersecurity researchers. Research firms say Pyongyang used watering holes to target banks in Mexico, Poland and Asia in 2016, leading to security improvements by those institutions and antivirus software firms.

> **North Korea's hacking program dates at least to the mid-1990s, when then-leader Kim Jong Il said that "all wars in future years will be computer wars."**

North Korea re-emerged last June with a watering hole variant that uses different encryptions and commands, according to cybersecurity firm Proofpoint Inc., which named the malware PowerRatankba.

The adaptation "shows that North Korea can recover when a researcher finds their tooling, publishes on it and lets the world know how to stop it," says Ryan Kalember, a Proofpoint senior vice president. "They are developing their own tools with a software-development life cycle, making products and improving them over time."

North Korea's hacking program dates at least to the mid-1990s, when then-leader Kim Jong Il said that "all wars in future years will be computer wars."

Its hacking made headlines in 2014 by knocking Sony Corp.'s Sony Pictures Entertainment's computer systems offline, erasing company data and pilfering troves of emails that eventually became public. The attack itself, cyber researchers now say, deployed an uncomplicated, widely available "wiper" tool.

Defectors and South Korea cyber experts say hacker trainees recruited by North Korea's government get roomy Pyongyang apartments and exemptions from mandatory military service.

The North Korean defector familiar with the country's cyber training says he received such training, and describes intense preparation for annual "hackathon" competitions in Pyongyang, in which teams of students holed up learning to solve puzzles and hacking problems under severe time pressure.

"For six months, day and night, we prepared only for this contest," he says. He recalls going home for a meal after an all-night prep session only to wake up with his head resting in his bowl of soup. "It was everyone's dream to be a part of it."

Top performers, he says, get jobs foraging for money via websites of overseas banks or targeting computer networks for intelligence in countries such as the U.S.

"To maintain the nuclear program and build more weapons and maintain the North Korean regime, a lot of hard currency is needed, so naturally attacking banks is of first importance," he says.

Some trainees are sent overseas to master foreign languages or to participate in international hackathons in places such as India or China, where they compete against coders from around the world. At a 2015 global competition called CodeChef, run by an Indian software company, North Korean teams ranked first, second and third out of more than 7,600 world-wide. Three of the top 15 coders in CodeChef's network of about 100,000 participants are North Korean.

The defectors and South Korean researchers say North Korea's cyber army has about 7,000 hackers and support staffers, loosely divided into three teams. The A team, often called "Lazarus" by foreign researchers, attacks foreign entities and is associated with North Korea's most headline-grabbing campaigns, such as the WannaCry and Sony attacks.

The B team traditionally focused on South Korea and swept for military or infrastructure secrets, though it has begun mining for intelligence elsewhere recently, the cyber researchers say. The C team does lower-skilled work, such as targeted email attacks called spear phishing.

While its earlier attacks used well-known tools and familiar coding, Pyongyang tried to learn from better hackers abroad, says Simon Choi, a cybersecurity consultant to South Korea's government who tracks online behavior. North Korean-linked accounts on Facebook and Twitter began following famous Chinese hackers and marked "like" on pages of how-to books outlining how to make malicious code for mobile devices, he says. Some North Koreans registered for online courses offered in South Korea teaching people how to hack smartphones, he says.

North Korea has planted programmers abroad where they can more easily connect online with the global financial system, security firms say. Recorded Future Inc., an intelligence firm, says it has tracked cyber activities with North Korean fingerprints to places such as China, India, New Zealand and Mozambique.

McAfee said it took suspected North Korean cyberwarriors just seven days in December to discover and use Invoke-PSImage, a new open-source hacking tool, to target groups involved in the Winter Olympics. McAfee said hackers used the tool to custom-build a malware download that was invisible to most antivirus software and hid malicious files in an image attached to a Word document.

Researchers say they were particularly impressed with the recent attack that capitalized on previously unknown vulnerabilities with Adobe Flash. According to South Korean and U.S. cyber researchers, the malware popped up in November targeting South Koreans, attaching itself to Microsoft Office files distributed by email. Victims infected their computers by viewing embedded Adobe Flash content in Word documents or spreadsheets. Hackers were then able to gain remote access to those PCs and steal files.

Adobe put out a security advisory on Feb. 1 and released a software patch five days later. FireEye said it suspected the malware came from North Korean hackers.

Within weeks, suspected Pyongyang hackers had adapted the original malware, which then appeared in attacks on financial institutions in Turkey in early March, according to McAfee. Although no money was taken, the attacks likely obtained intelligence, possibly including details of how the banks' internal systems work, McAfee said.

"This malware was not written by some average Joe," says Christian Beek, McAfee's senior principal engineer.

Mr. Choi, the South Korean cyber consultant, digitally pursued the author of the malware, piecing together details from the attack to gather biographical details. He eventually found what he believes is the male hacker's Facebook page. The listed hometown and current city was Pyongyang.

Print Citations

CMS: Martin, Timothy W. "How North Korea's Hackers Became Dangerously Good." In *The Reference Shelf: The Two Koreas*, edited by Micah L. Issit, 56-61. Ipswich, MA: H.W. Wilson, 2019.

MLA: Martin, Timothy W. "How North Korea's Hackers Became Dangerously Good." *The Reference Shelf: The Two Koreas,* edited by Micah L. Issit, H.W. Wilson, 2019, pp. 56-61.

APA: Martin, T.W. (2019). How North Korea's hackers became dangerously good. In Micah L. Issit (Ed.), *The reference shelf: The two Koreas* (pp. 56-61). Ipswich, MA: H.W. Wilson.

Reminder: North Korea Is Still Very Much a Nuclear Threat

By Ryan Bort
Rolling Stone, November 12, 2018

Earlier this year, a handful of congressmen formally nominated President Trump for the Nobel Peace Prize. "Although North Korea has evaded demands from the international community to cease its aggression for decades, President Trump's peace through strength policies are working and bringing peace to the Korean Peninsula," the letter concluded, anticipating the president's June summit with Kim Jong-un. But the Nobel committee was unmoved by Trump glad-handing a murderous dictator, and ultimately awarded the prize to Nadia Murad, an activist for those who survived sexual abuse at the hands of ISIS, and Denis Mukwege, a gynecological surgeon from the Congo.

Trump has complained as recently as late October that he likely will never win the Nobel Peace Prize. "They probably never will give it to me, even with what I'm doing in Korea and Idlib province and all of these places," the president said while gesturing wildly during a speech given to the Future Farmers of America. "They probably will never give it to me. You know why? Because they don't want to!"

The real reason Trump will never get the Nobel Peace Prize is that he isn't actually doing anything in North Korea. His meeting with Kim this past summer was widely regarded as a disaster, with the president legitimizing the world's most dangerous autocrat on a global stage while securing nothing for the United States other than the returned remains of Korean War veterans and a vague promise to denuclearize. But Trump really likes Kim—in fact, he loves him—so the president decided to go ahead and take at his work the man leading a regime that has been lying to the United States for years about plans to disarm.

Donald J. Trump
@realDonaldTrump

Just landed—a long trip, but everybody can now feel much safer than the day I took office. There is no longer a Nuclear Threat from North Korea. Meeting with Kim Jong Un was an interesting and very positive experience. North Korea has great potential for the future!

But on Monday the *New York Times* reported that North Korea's ballistic missile program is very much active, and that satellite images have identified 16 hidden bases across the peninsula. "The satellite images suggest that the North has been engaged in a great deception," the *Times* notes. "It has offered to dismantle a major launching site—a step it began, then halted—while continuing to make improvements at more than a dozen others that would bolster launches of conventional and nuclear warheads."

The *Times* goes on to point out that after Democrats gained control of the House of Representatives last Tuesday, Trump said that there was "no rush" to resume talks with North Korea as, again, he believes the situation has already resolved itself. This could prove to be a major problem, as Trump has demonstrated that once he's made up his mind about something—like, say, climate change being a hoax—he isn't very open to contrary views. If curtailing North Korea's nuclear weapons program isn't a priority for Trump, it probably isn't going to be as much as a priority as it should be for government agencies who are increasingly beholden to indulging the president's uninformed whims. The *Times* point out that U.S. intelligence has "long known" of North Korea's network of operational missile bases, but that it has been "left undiscussed as President Trump claims to have neutralized the North's nuclear threat."

By not addressing the threat, the Trump administration is enabling it. Trump has falsely and repeatedly claimed that the United States was on the brink of war with North Korea under President Obama. It was Obama, though, whose administration authorized a plan to track the movements of North Korean missiles through "a new generation of small, inexpensive satellites" developed by Silicon Valley. The initiative has stalled under Trump.

Pretty much everyone other than the president recognizes that North Korea hasn't even begun to denuclearize, and doesn't seem to have any intention of doing so. They've rebuffed Secretary of State Mike Pompeo's efforts to continue talks, and have yet to provide the United States with any information about its nuclear program and how it plans to disarm. Trump is getting played by North Korea, and he's either too incompetent realize it or too proud to admit it. The tepid statement the State Department released in response to the *Times* report is about as tough of a stance as the administration will take toward Kim. "President Trump has made clear that should Chairman Kim follow through on his commitments, including complete denuclearization and the elimination of ballistic missile programs, a much brighter future lies ahead for North Korea and its people," a spokesperson said.

Victor Cha, the leader of the research team that produced the images revealing the operational missile sites, surmised North Korea's strategy in an interview the *Times*. "It's not like these bases have been frozen. Work is continuing. What everybody is worried about is that Trump is going to accept a bad deal—they give us a single test site and

> **Pretty much everyone other than the president recognizes that North Korea hasn't even begun to denuclearize, and doesn't seem to have any intention of doing so.**

dismantle a few other things, and in return they get a peace agreement," he said, adding that Trump would then "declare victory, say he got more than any other American president ever got, and the threat would still be there."

But Trump has already declared victory, and if he were to again meet with Kim, he would come out of that meeting doing it all over again. All of the things people assume Trump values most—wealth, class, fame—do not actually matter to the president; all that matters is the appearance of possessing those thing[s]. It's is all a big show, from his hair to world peace, and Trump is satisfied as long as he can convince people something is true. When he was a real estate developer, the worst that could happen when the facade fell apart was a few casinos going bankrupt. Now that he's the president of the United States, it's nuclear war. He doesn't seem to know the difference.

Print Citations

CMS: Bort, Ryan. "Reminder: North Korea Is Still Very Much a Nuclear Threat." In *The Reference Shelf: The Two Koreas*, edited by Micah L. Issit, 62-64. Ipswich, MA: H.W. Wilson, 2019.

MLA: Bort, Ryan. "Reminder: North Korea Is Still Very Much a Nuclear Threat." *The Reference Shelf: The Two Koreas*, edited by Micah L. Issit, H.W. Wilson, 2019, pp. 62-64.

APA: Bort, R. (2019). Reminder: North Korea is still very much a nuclear threat. In Micah L. Issit (Ed.), *The reference shelf: The two Koreas* (pp. 62-64). Ipswich, MA: H.W. Wilson.

North Korea Is Not the Threat Trump Would Have You Believe

By Isaac Stone Fish
The Atlantic, January 31, 2018

During his State of the Union address on Tuesday, President Donald Trump spent several minutes speaking about two men who suffered horrifically in North Korea. Trump told the well-known, tragic story of Otto Warmbier, a University of Virginia student arrested in January 2016 in North Korea for allegedly stealing a propaganda poster. Not long after Pyongyang sentenced him to 15 years of hard labor, Warmbier fell into a coma; he died in the United States on June 19, 2017, six days after North Korea released him. "You are powerful witnesses to a menace that threatens our world," Trump said to the nation and to Warmbier's family, who sat in the audience. Trump then introduced 34-year-old North Korean Ji Seong Ho, who survived torture, starvation, and a crippling train accident before defecting in 2006. He is a "witness to the ominous nature of this regime," Trump said.

Trump cited Warmbier and Ji to personalize Pyongyang's iniquities, and, possibly, plant the emotional seeds for a military strike against North Korea. And yet, Ji and Warmbier's experiences represent radically different facets of the regime: how it treats its own citizens, versus how it treats Americans. Ji's experience in North Korea, while extraordinary, is not singular. His grandmother starved to death in the mid-90s, amid a famine that killed thousands, if not millions. Authorities tortured Ji after he returned from a trip to China, just as they've tortured thousands of his compatriots, including many of the more than 100,000 people Amnesty International estimates languish in four of North Korea's known political prison camps.

Unlike Ji's experience, Warmbier's is unique, and not representative. Of the thousands of Americans who have visited North Korea since the death of the country's longtime leader Kim Il Sung in 1994, Warmbier is the only one known to have died from injuries suffered there. Americans who visit North Korea—I've spoken to dozens of them over the last decade, and have been there twice myself—experience a level of luxury unimaginable to many North Koreans. They eat to satiation, sleep in air-conditioned hotels, and face very little risk of molestation from the North Korean secret service.

The same dichotomy exists on the international stage as well. Pyongyang poses an existential threat to the psychological, spiritual, emotional, and physical health of its citizens, and to the North Korean nation. But despite what Kim may be intending with his bombastic rhetoric, his regime poses a surprisingly small threat to the United States. That's not what you'll hear from Trump, however. "We need only look at the depraved character of the North Korean regime to understand the nature of the nuclear threat it could pose to America and our allies," he said in his address last night. But such declarations conflate the threat Pyongyang poses to its own people with the threat it poses to Americans. Trump "makes the fundamental mistake of equating brutal regimes with undeterrable regimes," tweeted Vipin Narang, a nuclear proliferation expert at the Massachusetts Institute of Technology. "The two have nothing to do with each other." While the United States has no good options on North Korea, there are many steps it can take that are smarter, safer, and more beneficial to its interests than military action. These include diplomacy, burden-sharing with China, or even Barack Obama's studiously inactive "strategic patience" approach.

What, then, is the threat that North Korea poses to the United States? It's not that it will attack the United States or kill visiting Americans. It is that Washington will hype the Pyongyang menace to such a degree that Americans will come to believe North Korea actually *does* pose an existential threat to the United States, and feel compelled to act accordingly, risking the lives of millions of people in the first great war of the 21st century.

> **The Trump administration and many in Congress are creating a cartoonish image of Pyongyang as a suicidal rogue state bent on world destruction, rather than as a desperately poor nation that abuses its citizens.**

That, sadly, seems to be the direction America is heading. In the summer of 2017, following the death of the 22-year-old Warmbier, the State Department banned U.S. passport holders from visiting the country without first receiving special permission. Besides encouraging Americans to believe North Korea is a dangerous place to visit, that move also ended one of the few channels Americans had for interacting with actual North Koreans. One tourist I spoke with who joined Warmbier on his fateful tour, and who asked to remain anonymous so that he could speak frankly, described how the experience humanized North Koreans for him, and vice versa. These encounters are maybe the only "kind of representation these people get of Americans that is not this cartoonish devil caricature," he told me.

In August, after the Kim regime threatened to retaliate against America for new UN sanctions against the country, Trump warned that North Korea "will be met with fire, fury and frankly power the likes of which this world has never seen before." The United States would have been better off if Trump ignored its comments: Pyongyang often pretends it will respond with aggression to situations it winds up ignoring. Pyongyang, for example, has considered so many things to be a "declaration of war" over the last two decades that in 2006, *The Onion* satirized the country's then-leader with the headline "Kim Jong Il Interprets Sunrise as Act of War."

On January 10, the State Department took things even further. Americans who receive permission to visit North Korea should "draft a will and designate appropriate insurance beneficiaries and/or power of attorney," it wrote on its travel warnings website. And those Americans, State continued—in hyperbolic language it uses nowhere else on its website—should "discuss a plan with loved ones regarding care/custody of children, pets, property, belongings, non-liquid assets (collections, artworks, etc.), funeral wishes, etc." Pyongyang, where surveillance is pervasive, is far safer for Americans than, say, Caracas. Venezuela's capital, by some measures, has the highest murder rate in the world. And yet, the State Department merely suggests Americans "reconsider" travel to Venezuela.

Three days later on January 13—in an event that, for many Americans, underscored the threat posed by North Korea—the state of Hawaii's emergency alert system mistakenly warned of a "ballistic missile threat" to the islands. Many people assumed the non-existent missile came from Pyongyang. "The whole state was terrified," Hawaii Senator Brian Schatz said.

In a further sign of how close this administration may be to war, on January 30, the *Washington Post* reported that the White House no longer wanted the respected and hawkish Korea hand Victor D. Cha to serve as its ambassador to South Korea. Why? In part because he isn't hawkish enough: Cha disagreed with the White House's plan to launch a limited strike on North Korea to deter it from its nuclear weapons program.

And yet, the odds of North Korea launching a preemptive strike on the United States remain vanishingly slim. If North Korea "launched an unprovoked nuclear strike against the United States," said Kingston Reif, the director for Disarmament and Threat Reduction Policy at the nonpartisan Arms Control Association, "that would be suicide" for them. The very rare exception would be if Pyongyang feared, even with its nuclear weapons, that the United States posed an existential threat. If North Korea believed "a U.S. attack is imminent, either due to accurate intelligence or miscalculation," it might use nuclear weapons first "out of fear that its forces won't last long against the combined might" of the United States and South Korea, Reif said.

Through its escalating public threats, and by conflating Warmbier's experience with that of North Koreans like Ji, the Trump administration and many in congress are creating a cartoonish image of Pyongyang as a suicidal rogue state bent on world destruction, rather than as a desperately poor nation that abuses its citizens. And sadly for North Koreans like Ji, the regime uses the idea of a looming American attack to justify its existence.

The North Korean threat is becoming a self-fulfilling prophecy. The more Trump calls for the destruction of North Korea and acts as if the United States will attack the country, the more likely it becomes that Pyongyang will feel it has no choice but to deter the United States from acting, and the more support its citizens will feel for a government they think is protecting them from the threat of an American attack. In other words, the more Trump hypes the North Korea threat, the more real it becomes.

Print Citations

CMS: Fish, Isaac Stone. "North Korea Is Not the Threat Trump Would Have You Believe." In *The Reference Shelf: The Two Koreas*, edited by Micah L. Issit, 65-68. Ipswich, MA: H.W. Wilson, 2019.

MLA: Fish, Isaac Stone. "North Korea Is Not the Threat Trump Would Have You Believe." *The Reference Shelf: The Two Koreas,* edited by Micah L. Issit, H.W. Wilson, 2019, pp. 65-68.

APA: Fish, I.S. (2019). North Korea is not the threat Trump would have you believe. In Micah L. Issit (Ed.), *The reference shelf: The two Koreas* (pp. 65-68). Ipswich, MA: H.W. Wilson.

North Korea Rouses Neighbors to Reconsider Nuclear Weapons

By David E. Sanger, Choe Sang-Hun, and Motoko Rich
The New York Times, October 28, 2017

As North Korea races to build a weapon that for the first time could threaten American cities, its neighbors are debating whether they need their own nuclear arsenals.

The North's rapidly advancing capabilities have scrambled military calculations across the region, and doubts are growing the United States will be able to keep the atomic genie in the bottle.

For the first time in recent memory, there is a daily argument raging in both South Korea and Japan—sometimes in public, more often in private—about the nuclear option, driven by worry that the United States might hesitate to defend the countries if doing so might provoke a missile launched from the North at Los Angeles or Washington.

In South Korea, polls show 60 percent of the population favors building nuclear weapons. And nearly 70 percent want the United States to reintroduce tactical nuclear weapons for battlefield use, which were withdrawn a quarter-century ago.

There is very little public support for nuclear arms in Japan, the only nation ever to suffer a nuclear attack, but many experts believe that could reverse quickly if North and South Korea both had arsenals.

Prime Minister Shinzo Abe has campaigned for a military buildup against the threat from the North, and Japan sits on a stockpile of nuclear material that could power an arsenal of 6,000 weapons. Last Sunday, he won a commanding majority in parliamentary elections, fueling his hopes of revising the nation's pacifist Constitution.

This brutal calculus over how to respond to North Korea is taking place in a region where several nations have the material, the technology, the expertise and the money to produce nuclear weapons.

Beyond South Korea and Japan, there is already talk in Australia, Myanmar, Taiwan and Vietnam about whether it makes sense to remain nuclear-free if others arm themselves—heightening fears that North Korea could set off a chain reaction in which one nation after another feels threatened and builds the bomb.

In a recent interview, Henry A. Kissinger, one of the few nuclear strategists from the early days of the Cold War still living, said he had little doubt where things were headed.

"If they continue to have nuclear weapons," he said of North Korea, "nuclear weapons must spread in the rest of Asia."

"It cannot be that North Korea is the only Korean country in the world that has nuclear weapons, without the South Koreans trying to match it. Nor can it be that Japan will sit there," he added. "So therefore we're talking about nuclear proliferation."

Such fears have been raised before, in Asia and elsewhere, without materializing, and the global consensus against the spread of nuclear weapons is arguably stronger than ever.

But North Korea is testing America's nuclear umbrella—its commitment to defend its allies with nuclear weapons if necessary—in a way no nation has in decades. Similar fears of abandonment in the face of the Soviet Union's growing arsenal helped lead Britain and France to go nuclear in the 1950s.

President Trump, who leaves Nov. 3 for a visit to Asia, has intensified these insecurities in the region. During his presidential campaign, he spoke openly of letting Japan and South Korea build nuclear arms even as he argued they should pay more to support the American military bases there.

"There is going to be a point at which we just can't do this anymore," he told the *New York Times* in March 2016. Events, he insisted, were pushing both nations toward their own nuclear arsenals anyway.

Mr. Trump has not raised that possibility in public since taking office. But he has rattled the region by engaging in bellicose rhetoric against North Korea and dismissing talks as a "waste of time."

In Seoul and Tokyo, many have already concluded that North Korea will keep its nuclear arsenal, because the cost of stopping it will be too great—and they are weighing their options.

Capability to Build the Bomb

Long before North Korea detonated its first nuclear device, several of its neighbors secretly explored going nuclear themselves.

Japan briefly considered building a "defensive" nuclear arsenal in the 1960s despite its pacifist Constitution. South Korea twice pursued the bomb in the 1970s and 1980s, and twice backed down under American pressure. Even Taiwan ran a covert nuclear program before the United States shut it down.

Today, there is no question that both South Korea and Japan have the material and expertise to build a weapon.

All that is stopping them is political sentiment and the risk of international sanctions. Both nations signed the Nuclear Nonproliferation Treaty, but it is unclear how severely other countries would punish two of the world's largest economies for violating the agreement.

South Korea has 24 nuclear reactors and a huge stockpile of spent fuel from which it can extract plutonium—enough for more than 4,300 bombs, according to a 2015 paper by Charles D. Ferguson, then president of the Federation of American Scientists.

Japan once pledged never to stockpile more nuclear fuel than it can burn off. But it has never completed the necessary recycling and has 10 tons of plutonium stored domestically and another 37 tons overseas.

"We keep reminding the Japanese of their pledge," said Ernest J. Moniz, chief executive of the Nuclear Threat Initiative and an energy secretary in the Obama administration, noting that it would take years if not decades for Japan to consume its fissile material because almost all its nuclear plants have remained offline since the 2011 Fukushima accident.

China, in particular, has objected to Japan's stockpile, warning that its traditional rival is so advanced technologically that it could use the material to quickly build a large arsenal.

Analysts often describe Japan as a "de facto" nuclear state, capable of building a weapon within a year or two. "Building a physical device is not that difficult anymore," said Tatsujiro Suzuki, former deputy chairman of the Japan Atomic Energy Commission.

> In Seoul and Tokyo, many have already concluded that North Korea will keep its nuclear arsenal, because the cost of stopping it will be too great—and they are weighing their options.

Japan already possesses long-range missile technology, he added, but would need some time to develop more sophisticated communications and control systems.

South Korea may be even further along, with a fleet of advanced missiles that carry conventional warheads. In 2004, the government disclosed that its scientists had dabbled in reprocessing and enriching nuclear material without first informing the International Atomic Energy Agency as required by treaty.

"If we decide to stand on our own feet and put our resources together, we can build nuclear weapons in six months," said Suh Kune-yull, a professor of nuclear engineering at Seoul National University. "The question is whether the president has the political will."

In Seoul, a Rising Call for Arms

President Moon Jae-in has been firm in his opposition to nuclear weapons. He insists that building them or reintroducing American ones to South Korea would make it even more difficult to persuade North Korea to scrap its own.

Though Mr. Moon has received high approval ratings since his election in May, his view is increasingly a minority one.

Calls for nuclear armament used to be dismissed as chatter from South Korea's nationalist fringe. Not anymore. Now people often complain that South Korea cannot depend on the United States, its protector of seven decades.

The opposition Liberty Korea party called on the United States to reintroduce tactical nuclear weapons to South Korea in August after the North tested an intercontinental ballistic missile that appeared capable of reaching the mainland United States.

"If the U.N. Security Council can't rein in North Korea with its sanctions, we will have no option but to withdraw from the Nonproliferation Treaty," Won Yoo-chul, a party leader, said in September.

Given the failure of sanctions, threats and negotiations to stop North Korea, South Koreans are increasingly convinced the North will never give up its nuclear weapons. But they also oppose risking a war with a military solution.

Most believe the Trump administration, despite its tough talk, will ultimately acquiesce, perhaps settling for a freeze that allows the North to keep a small arsenal. And many fear that would mean giving the North the ultimate blackmail tool—and a way to keep

"The reason North Korea is developing a hydrogen bomb and intercontinental ballistic missiles is not to go to war with the United States," said Cheong Seong-chang, an analyst at the Sejong Institute near Seoul. "It's to stop the Americans from intervening in armed skirmishes or full-scale war on the Korean Peninsula."

The closer the North gets to showing it can strike the United States, the more nervous South Koreans become about being abandoned. Some have asked whether Washington will risk the destruction of an American city by intervening, for example, if the North attempts to occupy a border island, as its soldiers have practiced.

For many in South Korea, the solution is a homegrown nuclear deterrent.

"If we don't respond with our own nuclear deterrence of some kind, our people will live like nuclear hostages of North Korea," said Cheon Seong-whun, a former presidential secretary for security strategy.

With nuclear weapons of its own, the South would gain leverage and could force North Korea back to the bargaining table, where the two sides could whittle down their arsenals through negotiations, some hawks argue.

But given the risks of going nuclear, others say Seoul should focus on persuading Washington to redeploy tactical nuclear weapons.

"The redeployment of American tactical nuclear weapons would be the surest way" to deter North Korea, Defense Minister Song Young-moo said last month, but he added that it would be difficult to get Washington to agree to that

In Tokyo, Cautious Debate

The discussion in Japan has been more subdued than in South Korea, no surprise after 70 years of public education about the horrors of Hiroshima and Nagasaki.

But Japan has periodically considered developing nuclear weapons every decade since the 1960s.

In 2002, a top aide to Junichiro Koizumi, the prime minister then, caused a furor by suggesting Japan might one day break with its policy of never building, possessing or allowing nuclear arms on its territory.

North Korea has reopened that question.

Shigeru Ishiba, a former defense minister seen as a potential challenger to Prime Minister Abe, has argued that Japan needs to debate its nuclear policy given the threat from North Korea.

Mr. Abe has stopped short of calling for a re-evaluation of the country's position on nuclear weapons. But he has increased military spending and echoed Mr. Trump's hawkish position against the North.

Mr. Abe's administration has already determined that nuclear weapons would not be prohibited under the Constitution if maintained only for self-defense.

The Japanese public is largely opposed to nuclear weapons with polls indicating fewer than one in 10 support nuclear armament.

But Japan's relations with South Korea have long been strained, and if Seoul armed itself, those numbers could shift.

Some analysts say the discussion is aimed at getting additional reassurance from Washington. "We always do that when we become a little upset about the credibility of the extended U.S. deterrence," said Narushige Michishita, a professor at the National Graduate Institute for Policy Studies in Tokyo.

Tobias Harris, a Japan analyst at Teneo Intelligence, a political risk consultancy, said Japan would rethink its position on nuclear weapons if it suspects the United States would let it down.

"We're kind of in uncharted waters as far as this goes," he said. "It's hard to know exactly what the threshold is that will lead the Japanese public's switch to flip."

Print Citations

CMS: Sanger, David E., Choe Sang-Hun, and Motoko Rich. "North Korea Rouses Neighbors to Reconsider Nuclear Weapons." In *The Reference Shelf: The Two Koreas*, edited by Micah L. Issit, 69-73. Ipswich, MA: H.W. Wilson, 2019.

MLA: Sanger, David E., Choe Sang-Hun, and Motoko Rich. "North Korea Rouses Neighbors to Reconsider Nuclear Weapons." *The Reference Shelf: The Two Koreas,* edited by Micah L. Issit, H.W. Wilson, 2019, pp. 69-73.

APA: Sanger, D.E., Choe, S.-H., & Rich, M. (2019). North Korea rouses neighbors to reconsider nuclear weapons. In Micah L. Issit (Ed.), *The reference shelf: The two Koreas* (pp. 69-73). Ipswich, MA: H.W. Wilson.

The North Korean Threat Beyond ICBMs

By Graham Allison

The Atlantic, **August 28, 2017**

From the moment that President Barack Obama told President-elect Donald Trump during the transition about the impending threat of North Korean nuclear-tipped ICBMs, Trump's basic stance has been: not on my watch. From his tweet of January 2 ("won't happen!") to his August statements that the U.S. military is "locked and loaded" to unleash "fire and fury" on North Korea if it threatens America, Trump has sought to draw a red line that makes it clear he will do whatever is necessary to halt North Korea's nuclear and missile programs—*before* they can target the continental United States.

This, of course, would pose a huge, possibly intolerable threat. Once North Korea achieved the ability to strike San Francisco or Los Angeles, it would undoubtedly continue extending its reach to the rest of the United States. At that point, Americans would have to try to live with a formidable nuclear power that, like Russia or China, could kill tens of millions in the event of all-out war. And while the United States would build up missile defenses in the hope of limiting damage and bolster its nuclear deterrent, allowing such a regime to acquire such a capability will strike most Americans as unacceptable—if there is any other realistic alternative.

But to properly assess the nuclear threat posed by North Korea, Americans must first recognize the danger that its current arsenal of up to 60 nuclear weapons already poses to the United States and its allies. Kim Jong Un can already deliver a nuclear warhead against South Korea, where nearly 28,500 U.S. servicemen are based and nearly 200,000 U.S. citizens live; it can already hit Japan with a nuclear warhead, where close to 90,000 Americans live, including 39,000 U.S. troops. On Monday, alarm bells sounded in Japan when a North Korean missile overflew its northern provinces.

ICBMs, of course, have one fatal flaw: They leave an unambiguous return address. Kim Jong Un knows that within minutes of any launch of an ICBM against the United States, he and his regime will be toast. As Colin Powell once put it, the U.S. response would turn that country into a "charcoal briquette."

However, there is another, even more likely way that a North Korean nuclear weapon could explode in a U.S. city: Kim could sell one to terrorists. Are the terrorists the United States is fighting today interested in nuclear weapons? Ayman al-Zawahiri, the current leader of al Qaeda, has been seeking nuclear weapons for more than a decade. Moreover, in 2016, an ISIS-related group was discovered actively pursuing nuclear materials at a Belgian nuclear power plant. Does Kim imagine he could get away with selling a nuclear weapon, or the material to make one, to a terrorist group? One would think not—and the United States must do everything possible to make him believe that.

But no one can erase the fact that Pyongyang has already crossed that line without suffering serious consequences. Beginning in 2001, North Korea sold materials, designs, and expertise to Syria that helped it build a plutonium-producing nuclear reactor. By now, that reactor would have produced enough plutonium for several nuclear bombs—had it not been destroyed by an Israeli airstrike in 2007.

What price did North Korea pay? Pyongyang got its money; Syria was bombed; and the United States was soon back at the negotiating table in the six-party talks trying, unsuccessfully, to get North Korea to give up its nuclear weapons. North Korea is known in intelligence circles as "Missiles 'R' Us," having sold and delivered missiles to Iran, Syria, Pakistan, and others. As former secretary of defense Robert Gates said, the North Koreans will "sell anything they have to anybody who has the cash to buy it." Perversely, as the United States pushes for tighter enforcement of UN sanctions on North Korea, the cash-strapped regime has greater incentives to turn back to the nuclear black market.

To address the ICBM threat in the narrow window before Kim develops an operational capability, the Trump administration has expressed a readiness to negotiate on the condition that North Korea freezes nuclear and missile tests. Such a freeze would be a significant improvement over North Korea's relentless nuclear advance. But even if the Trump administration succeeds in stopping Kim at this point, the United States will then be left with all the dangers posed by Kim's existing nuclear stockpile. In addition, North Korea has facilities currently producing

> To properly assess the nuclear threat posed by North Korea, Americans must first recognize the danger that its current arsenal of up to 60 nuclear weapons already poses to the United States and its allies.

both plutonium and highly enriched uranium, which experts estimate can produce enough fissile material for 12 additional weapons per year. So the United States should also seek a freeze of North Korea's production of fissile materials.

In addition to the current effort, Trump needs to send Kim a clear message, with an identical copy delivered to China's president Xi Jinping: If any nuclear bomb of North Korean origin were to explode on American soil or that of an American ally, the United States will respond as though North Korea itself had hit the United States with a nuclear-tipped ICBM.

The recent "war of words" between Trump and Kim has awakened many Americans to the North Korean nuclear threat. While Americans can hope that the current confrontation will succeed in stopping further ICBM and nuclear tests, even if this succeeds, the United States will be left trying to live with the clear and present danger posed by a nuclear North Korea.

Print Citations

CMS: Allison, Graham. "The North Korean Threat Beyond ICBMs." In *The Reference Shelf: The Two Koreas*, edited by Micah L. Issit, 74-76. Ipswich, MA: H.W. Wilson, 2019.

MLA: Allison, Graham. "The North Korean Threat Beyond ICBMs." *The Reference Shelf: The Two Koreas,* edited by Micah L. Issit, H.W. Wilson, 2019, pp. 74-76.

APA: Allison, G. (2019). The North Korean threat beyond ICBMs. In Micah L. Issit (Ed.), *The reference shelf: The two Koreas* (pp. 74-76). Ipswich, MA: H.W. Wilson.

How Would the U.S. Defend against a North Korean Nuclear Attack?

By Chloe Whiteaker, Jeremy Scott Diamond, and Tony Capaccio
Bloomberg News, September 8, 2017

After successfully testing two intercontinental ballistic missiles and a bomb with far more destructive power than those dropped on Hiroshima and Nagasaki, the North Korean nuclear threat has never been more credible. When asked on Wednesday about possible military action, President Donald Trump said, "We'll see what happens." That did little to reassure those still shaken by his remarks last month that the U.S. military was "locked and loaded" and that further threats from Pyongyang would be met with "fire and fury." Secretary of State Rex Tillerson, for his part, is still pushing for a diplomatic solution and hoping to calm fears of nuclear war, saying "Americans should sleep well at night." But should we?

The U.S. missile defense system is a global network with 24-hour surveillance by land-, sea- and space-based sensors, all of which are constantly looking for signs of anything amiss in North Korea. Regional missile interceptors are deployed in Japan, South Korea, Guam and on U.S. Navy ships, while military bases in Alaska and California are equipped to intercept a missile headed toward the United States. So what would that response look like? It's impossible to say exactly, with so many variables in play and almost as many failures as successes in tests, but this is theoretically how the system should work.

If North Korea were to launch a missile, U.S. satellites would detect it almost instantaneously through infrared signals. In less than a minute, the satellite would raise the alarm, and the command and control center at Schriever Air Force Base near Colorado Springs, Colorado would spring into action.

The command center in Colorado would direct the radars in the region to track the missile as it climbed toward outer space. During that five- to seven-minute stretch, the TPY-2 and SPY-1 radar systems would be gathering data like trajectory, velocity and altitude to send back to the command center so they can figure out what type of missile was launched and whether it could reach the U.S. This "boost phase" is actually the ideal time to intercept a missile, but the current defense system isn't equipped to do so yet.

The officers at the command center would consult with U.S. Northern Command (Northcom), based nearby at Peterson Air Force Base, where a round-the-clock watch officer would be responsible for approving an interceptor launch. If there was time, they might notify the Secretary of Defense in Washington, too.

The command center would send launch orders after determining whether Fort Greely or Vandenberg Air Force Base was better-positioned to intercept. By the time of launch, about eight to ten minutes may have passed since the North Korean missile was first detected.

Ground-Based Interceptors (GBIs) are the only weapon capable of destroying an intercontinental ballistic missile (ICBM), and they've only been tested against such a missile once—with success. The U.S. only has 36 GBIs in the field—four in California and 32 in Alaska—and would likely launch a few per incoming missile to improve the odds of success during an attack. That stockpile is expected to expand to 44 by the end of the year, but it's not hard to imagine how the U.S. defense could theoretically be overpowered if North Korea were to fire multiple missiles. The Pentagon said in June that it can protect the nation from "a small number" of missiles—not a barrage

Once in space, the interceptor would release an Exoatmospheric Kill Vehicle (EKV)—a device that uses kinetic force to destroy missiles outside the Earth's atmosphere.

Radars would track both the EKV and the missile, looking out for countermeasures like decoys that some missiles use to confuse the defense. The TPY-2 and sea-based X-band radars are best at picking out a warhead from other flying objects in a so-called "threat cloud." Real-time updates would flow through the command center and be relayed to the EKV to guide it toward the incoming warhead.

Still flying through space, a North Korean warhead might be about three-quarters of the way through its roughly 30-minute journey to the U.S. at this point.

Using sensors, rocket thrusters and guidance from the command center, the EKV may fly for roughly six to 12 minutes before hurtling itself into the warhead at incredible speed—completely destroying it and avoiding nuclear catastrophe.

To be sure, the whole process could happen quicker, but without history to reference, estimates are the best information available. Experts say there are countless variables that could shift the clock one way or the other—trajectory, altitude and targets to name a few.

Intercepting a missile is commonly compared to hitting a bullet with another bullet. How often does that actually work? In 18 tests since 1999, ten have been successful. Only one—on May 30—was against an ICBM. None included multiple missile threats. Critics lambast the tests for being unrealistic and scripted to ensure success—they're conducted with few decoys and in daylight with advanced warning.

"The tests are reflective of what we're seeing in the threat," according to Ian Williams at the Center for Strategic and International Studies. More recent tests have included some decoys and dodging maneuvers. Next year the Pentagon will launch two interceptors at one target for the first time.

Testing interceptors to make sure the $36 billion system works in a realistic scenario is understandably difficult—not least of all because the Pentagon must ensure the interception occurs in a carefully crafted location that is clear of populated areas or ships beneath it, should debris fall down to Earth. It's costly

A redesigned kill vehicle is expected by 2020, which promises easier and cheaper production while also improving reliability.

too—the May 30 test cost $244 million. That said, "they're on the right track in the fixes" but haven't yet proven a "realistic capability," according to Laura Grego, senior scientist for the Global Security Program at the Union of Concerned Scientists.

More improvements are on the way. A redesigned kill vehicle is expected by 2020, which promises easier and cheaper production while also improving reliability. A multi-object kill vehicle is in development, with talks of accelerating the program, which would allow sending more than one kill vehicle on a single GBI. Congress is also pushing to increase the number of GBIs in deployment. An amendment to the defense policy bill for fiscal 2018, proposed by Senator Dan Sullivan (R-Alaska), would add another 28 GBIs—to bring the total up to 72—and explore options for increasing the reserves to 100. That bill also calls for a new space-based sensor layer that would provide precision-tracking of missiles and more advanced discrimination between warheads and debris.

On the ground, a new high-resolution, long-range discrimination radar (LRDR) is scheduled to be deployed by the end of 2020 and would have a much wider, clearer view for tracking missiles to improve the accuracy of the GBIs we have. There's been support in Congress for a third missile defense site in the eastern U.S. as well, though top officials at the Missile Defense Agency and the Pentagon have said it's not really necessary because the current sites already protect all 50 states.

What's more, some experts believe North Korea is still a ways off from being able to back up its threats. "It is clear North Korea has the capability to build a missile that can range the distance to the United States, but North Korea has yet to demonstrate it has the requisite technology and capability to actually target and strike the United States with a nuclear weapon," according to General Paul Selva, the No. 2 U.S. military official, who offered his thoughts in a statement to Bloomberg on Aug. 29. In the end, all sides would like to see that the missile defense system never needs to be used at all.

So should Americans sleep well at night? Yes, for now.

Print Citations

CMS: Whiteaker, Chloe, Jeremy Scott Diamond, and Tony Capaccio. "How Would the U.S. Defend Against a North Korean Nuclear Attack?" In *The Reference Shelf: The Two Koreas*, edited by Micah L. Issit, 77-80. Ipswich, MA: H.W. Wilson, 2019.

MLA: Whiteaker, Chloe, Jeremy Scott Diamond, and Tony Capaccio. "How Would the U.S. Defend Against a North Korean Nuclear Attack?" *The Reference Shelf: The Two Koreas*, edited by Micah L. Issit, H.W. Wilson, 2019, pp. 77-80.

APA: Whiteaker, C., Diamond, J.S., & Capaccio, T. (2019). How would the U.S. defend against a North Korean nuclear attack? (2019). In Micah L. Issit (Ed.), *The reference shelf: The two Koreas* (pp. 77-80). Ipswich, MA: H.W. Wilson.

North Korea's Illegal Weapons Trade

By Bruce E. Bechtol, Jr.
Foreign Affairs, June 6, 2018

As U.S. President Donald Trump and North Korean Supreme Leader Kim Jong Un prepare for the first ever summit between the heads of their respective countries, it appears that, at least for now, the brinkmanship and threats we have seen in the recent past are at an end. Regardless of the fate of the summit, however, the United States and its allies will be forced to deal with North Korea's weapons programs, which now threaten not only U.S. allies such as South Korea and Japan but potentially the continental United States itself.

International attention in recent years has understandably centered on Pyongyang's advances in nuclear weapons technology and the question of whether North Korea can be convinced to denuclearize. This focus, however, has tended to obscure the fact that North Korea's military development serves two purposes. The first is the ability to intimidate and threaten both its neighbors in the region and the United States. The second, less well-known purpose is to proliferate weapons—conventional, unconventional, and weapons of mass destruction—to desperate and unstable regions around the world in exchange for hard currency.

For decades, North Korea has proliferated weapons, including conventional arms, ballistic missiles, and chemical agents, to states such as Iran and Syria (and by extension to their nonstate proxies), helping them to evade international sanctions and providing them with the necessary technical and military assistance to develop their own weapons programs.

The Syrian Connection

Perhaps the most visible instance of North Korean proliferation can be seen in Syria, where the regime of President Bashar al-Assad, largely financed by his patrons in Tehran, has purchased and deployed North Korean weapons against his own people throughout the course of the country's seven-year civil war.

North Korean–Syrian military relations go back to the 1960s, when both countries were part of the Soviet sphere of influence. North Korean pilots assisted the Syrian air force against Israel in the Six-Day War and Yom Kippur War, and during the First Lebanon War in 1982, North Korean special forces trained Syrian troops in guerrilla warfare. Throughout this relationship, Pyongyang has been a major supplier of conventional weapons to Damascus, including artillery, guns, tanks, and systems such as multiple-rocket launchers that have been used to deliver chemical weapons.

Since the end of the Cold War, North Korea has also been proliferating ballistic missiles to Syria. During the mid- to late 1990s, Pyongyang allegedly sold several hundred Scud-C missiles and missile production kits to Damascus. Beginning in the early years of the same decade, the North Koreans, in a pattern that continues to this day, contracted to build missile fabrication facilities for the Syrians. Instead of shipping whole missiles to Syria, that is, they would ship the parts—making it easier to evade sanctions—which would then be assembled in Syria with assistance from North Korean technicians. North Korea has also used this strategy to assist the Syrians in building and testing an advanced Scud-D.

North Korea has been deeply involved in Syria's chemical weapons program as well. In 2004, several Syrian technicians were killed in a train explosion in Ryongchon, North Korea. The Syrians, employees of the Syrian Scientific Studies and Research Center (the agency in charge of many of Syria's covert weapons of mass destruction programs), were accompanying a shipment of missiles and missile components to the North Korean port of Nampo, from which they would be sent to Syria. And since the beginning of Syria's civil war in 2011, cooperation between Damascus and Pyongyang has increased. According to reports from 2013, North Korea, Syria, and Iran have collaborated in the "planning, establishment, and management" of at least five Syrian facilities that manufacture precursors of chemical weapons. A UN Panel of Experts report from earlier this year revealed, among other things, that a North Korean technical delegation transferred thermometers and resistance valves for use in chemical weapons during an August 2016 visit to Syria; that North Korean ballistic missile technicians traveled to Syria in April and November 2016; and that North Korean missile and chemical technicians continue to work at facilities in Adra, Barzeh, and Hama.

North Korea has used a variety of tricks to make these sales in the face of international sanctions. Pyongyang has used sealed diplomatic shipments, which are normally not inspected, and foreign front companies to avoid interdiction. The Panel of Experts report identified 39 shipments from North Korea to Syria between 2012 and 2017, most of them sending arms, including chemical weapons. One member state informed the panel of a shipment from a North Korean front company that included grenade launchers, machine guns, and 30 mm autocannons. These are likely just the tip of the iceberg—during the same time period at least two states reported interdicting North Korean arms shipments to Syria, one of which included tiles used in the construction of new chemical weapons facilities.

> For decades, North Korea has proliferated weapons, including conventional arms, ballistic missiles, and chemical agents, to states such as Iran and Syria.

Some have said that North Korea's proliferation of nuclear weapons technology to other rogue states represents a redline, but that bridge has already been crossed.

In 2008, the year after the Israeli air force destroyed a suspected Syrian nuclear reactor in Deir ez-Zor, a briefing from the Office of the Director of National Intelligence definitively showed that Pyongyang was assisting Syria in building a copy of the plutonium reactor at Yongbyon, which North Korea has used to produce its own nuclear weapons. (The Deir ez-Zor facility would have been able to produce the same thing for the Syrians.) According to a high-ranking Iranian defector—Ali Reza Asghari, a former deputy defense minister—the construction of the reactor was financed by Iran, to the tune of some $2 billion, according to Israeli estimates. When it comes to Syria, North Korea has literally proliferated everything from rifles to a nuclear program to a troubled nation still divided by civil war.

Friends in Tehran

North Korea's best customer, however, is not Syria but Iran. The two states' relationship began in earnest during the Iran-Iraq War. By the end of the war in 1988, some 300 North Korean military advisers were on the ground in Iran, and Pyongyang had reportedly sold Tehran more than $1 billion in conventional arms, training, and military assistance.

Like Syria, Iran is a major purchaser of North Korean conventional weapons. Iran's Ghadir-class submarine, for instance, appears to be an exact replica of a North Korean submarine called the Yeono—the same model that sank a South Korean navy corvette in 2010. The Iranian–North Korean relationship, however, also extends to Iranian funding of weapons purchases by its regional proxies and allies, including Hezbollah, the Syrian government, Houthi rebels in Yemen, and Hamas in Gaza—many of which come from North Korea. According to Larry Niksch, a senior associate of the Center for Strategic and International Studies, "North Korea may receive from Iran upwards of $2 to $3 billion annually . . . for the various forms of collaboration between them." This estimate makes sense, particularly if one includes the many arms purchases for Syria and nonstate actors that Iran has made from Pyongyang in recent years. The Houthis have used North Korean ballistic missiles—probably Scuds captured from the Yemeni government—to threaten the Saudis and have also used longer-range variants of North Korean missiles, provided by Iran, to target Riyadh. In April, Israeli intelligence assassinated a Hamas engineer in Malaysia who was involved in negotiating an arms deal with Pyongyang.

Although conventional weapons are an important part of the Iranian–North Korean relationship, what is truly eye-catching is Iran's purchase of ballistic missile systems over the years. Iran began buying Scud-B missiles from North Korea in the mid-1980s for use against Iraq and started the process of acquiring Scud-C missiles soon thereafter, around 1990. The Scud-C purchases marked an important milestone: rather than selling the completed missiles, North Korea began setting up manufacturing and assembly facilities within Iran itself. These facilities have been the source of confusion among international analysts, since they allow Iran to claim that it is indigenously producing these weapons systems despite the fact that they cannot be made without assistance from, and parts manufactured in, North Korea.

In 1993, North Korea conducted its first known successful test launch of the Nodong—a test launch attended by Iranian officials. Soon afterward, in the mid-1990s, Iran began purchasing Nodongs using hard currency and possibly oil. In October 2015, the Iranians tested a missile called the Emad, which is essentially a Nodong with a slightly upgraded range—1,700 kilometers to the Nodong's 1,500—and an improved guidance system. The Emad was likely built with both assistance and parts from North Korea. During the early 1990s, the North Koreans were also able to obtain a complete Russian SS-N-6 ballistic missile system, allowing them to develop their own variant known as the Musudan—a more powerful (if more complicated) missile than the Nodong. In 2005, Pyongyang allegedly sold 18 Musudan missiles to Iran. And in January 2006, Tehran reportedly conducted a successful test launch of the Musudan. Analysis of the launch led to an assessed range of 4,000 kilometers.

In 2013, it was revealed that Iran and North Korea were collaborating on a new, 80-ton long-range rocket booster for an intercontinental ballistic missile (ICBM), and in 2015 reports emerged that Pyongyang had supplied Tehran with several shipments of missile components even as nuclear talks proceeded between Iran and the United States, with at least two shipments during the fall of 2015. In 2016, following North Korea's fourth nuclear test, the U.S. Treasury Department imposed sanctions on Iranian officials acting on behalf of the Shahid Hemmat Industrial Group and Iran's Ministry of Defense for Armed Forces Logistics, who had violated U.S. and UN sanctions by dealing with the Korea Mining Development Trading Corporation, one of North Korea's key front companies for weapons proliferation. Specifically, North Korean officials had visited Iran and Iranian officials had visited North Korea for contract negotiations regarding Iran's purchase of the ICBM rocket booster that had first been revealed in 2013. Iranian technicians also traveled to North Korea as the rocket booster was in development.

Murkier than the Iranian–North Korean ballistic missile connection is Pyongyang's relationship to Tehran's nuclear weapons program—although widely suspected, evidence has largely been limited to anecdotal reports in the press. A 2003 article in the *Los Angeles Times* by the veteran reporter Douglas Frantz reported Iranian contacts with China, Pakistan, Russia, and North Korea in pursuit of nuclear weapons capabilities. Most famous among these was the Pakistani scientist Abdul Qadeer Khan, but Frantz also reported that "so many North Koreans are working on nuclear and missile projects in Iran that a resort on the Caspian coast is set aside for their exclusive use." According to a January 2006 report by Robin Hughes in *Jane's Defense Weekly,* North Korea constructed more than 10,000 meters of underground nuclear facilities for Iran. In 2011, reports in the European press, suggested that North Korea had supplied Iran with a computer program simulating neutron flows and training for how to use it. And in November of that year, the *Washington Post,* citing intelligence provided to the International Atomic Energy Agency, reported that "Iran also relied on foreign experts to supply mathematical formulas and codes for theoretical design work [for its nuclear program]—some of which appear to have originated in North Korea."

How Washington Can Respond

Given the ongoing scale of North Korea's proliferation efforts, how should policy-makers in the United States and elsewhere respond? The Proliferation Security Initiative, an international effort to halt the trafficking of weapons of mass destruction initiated by U.S. President George W. Bush in 2003, is a good start and with increased allied support in the form of resources and personnel could make a dent in North Korea's illicit shipments.

There are two further ways to fight the North Korean arms trade. The first is to more effectively enforce existing U.S. and UN sanctions. Sanctions are no better than the paper they are printed on unless international law enforcement and diplomatic entities actively work to ensure that nations, banks, and front companies violating the sanctions face the full force of U.S. and international law. On the bright side, enforcement was stepped up last fall as a result of Trump's pressure campaign and is likely to constrain North Korea. The second is to use Section 311 of the U.S.A. Patriot Act, which empowers the U.S. Treasury Department to target terrorist financing, to go after banks, front companies, and individuals involved in North Korea's complicated illicit financial network. If actors working on behalf of Pyongyang can be pinpointed and excluded from access to U.S. and allied banks and financial institutions, this will severely limit North Korea's ability to sell and ship its weapons abroad.

The Trump administration has already taken important steps in the right direction. On September 21, 2017, Trump issued an executive order authorizing the Treasury Department to completely cut off North Korean access to the U.S. dollar and to sanction any person or entity attempting to do business with Pyongyang. The United States can—and likely will—go after banks and front companies in China, but it will also pursue them in places such as Singapore, Malaysia, and several countries in Africa.

North Korea has for many years been able to use the money it earns from military proliferation to pay for its nuclear and ballistic missile programs, oversize military, and subsidies for the elite that keeps Kim in power. As Trump prepares to meet with Kim, it would be good for him to learn from the mistakes of his predecessors, none of whom succeeded in disarming North Korea or containing its rogue-state behavior. The administration of George W. Bush, for instance, brought Pyongyang back to the bargaining table with an economic pressure campaign that effectively cut into the profits of North Korea's financial networks. But when it came time to dismantle its nuclear program, Pyongyang engaged in the "action for action" model, gaining concessions from the United States without in the end giving up any of its nuclear weapons program.

Washington must not repeat these mistakes. It would also be good to remember that verifiable steps are not dismantlement. Unless the United States is allowed to inspect all nuclear sites at the time of its choosing, and until it becomes clear that North Korea has completely dismantled its nuclear program, Washington must keep up the pressure on Pyongyang's illegal economic activities—proliferation key among them. Continued pursuit of North Korea's weapons trade and the financial networks that support it is not only the right thing to do but essential for giving Washington the leverage to pressure Pyongyang.

Print Citations

CMS: Bechtol, Bruce E. Jr. "North Korea's Illegal Weapons Trade." In *The Reference Shelf: The Two Koreas*, edited by Micah L. Issit, 81-86. Ipswich, MA: H.W. Wilson, 2019.

MLA: Bechtol, Bruce E. Jr. "North Korea's Illegal Weapons Trade." *The Reference Shelf: The Two Koreas,* edited by Micah L. Issit, H.W. Wilson, 2019, pp. 81-86.

APA: Bechtol, B.E. Jr. (2019). North Korea's illegal weapons trade. (2019). In Micah L. Issit (Ed.), *The reference shelf: The two Koreas* (pp. 81-86). Ipswich, MA: H.W. Wilson.

4
The Current Summit Talks and What They Mean for the Future

North Korean leader Kim Jong-Un and U.S. President Trump shake hands at the start of the 2018 North Korea-United States Summit, June 2018. Although talks between the two leaders have stalled since the summit, relations between North and South Korea are improving.

The Rhetorical War

President Trump and North Korean President Kim Jong-Un met on June 12, 2018, in Singapore in what has been called a historic meeting. In a press release following the meeting, Donald Trump claimed:

> Chairman Kim and I just signed a joint statement in which he reaffirmed his "unwavering commitment to complete denuclearization of the Korean Peninsula." We also agreed to vigorous negotiations to implement the agreement as soon as possible. And he wants to do that. This isn't the past. This isn't another administration that never got it started and therefore never got it done.[1]

Though touted as a victory by the Trump administration, in December of 2018, the DPRK released a statement claiming that they will not denuclearize until the United States eliminates what it characterizes as a "nuclear threat." Despite this, the summit played a role in fostering renewed talks between North and South Korea, and many national security analysts hope that these negotiations might deescalate tensions surrounding the buildup of North Korea's nuclear arsenal.[2]

A Long History of Failed Negotiations

One of the most globally impactful developments of the Cold War was the "nuclear arms race," a competition between the United States and Russia to develop and stockpile nuclear weapons and create or strengthen their international military reach and influence. By 1960, the size of the nuclear arsenals amassed by the United States and Russia, combined with military assistance treaties, meant that any nuclear war would be a globally devastating conflict. During this time, the United States was stockpiling weapons toward the goal of what was called "mutually assured destruction," a theory of deterrence based on the idea that neither side would attack because doing so would guarantee that both sides would be destroyed. Once both nations had achieved sufficient weapons to assure mutual destruction, diplomats began working on a way to halt or at least limit the continued buildup. This resulted in the Nuclear Non-Proliferation Treaty (NPT) of 1968, a series of international agreements between the United States, Russia, and other nuclear and non-nuclear nations in an effort to prevent future nuclear war. The NPT created the International Atomic Energy Agency (IAEA), which is empowered to conduct inspections to ensure that member countries are not secretly developing nuclear weapons technology.[3]

One of the ways in which the international community attempts to enforce the NPT is through the use of economic sanctions. The United States has utilized economic sanctions against North Korea since 1950, when they issued a complete embargo on any exports to the nation. These sanctions remained in place after the end of the war and, in the 1960s, were used as part of an effort to prevent North Korea from developing nuclear weapons.

Under the leadership of Kim Il-Sung, North Korea built its first nuclear facility in the 1980s, largely in response to the fact that the United States had placed nuclear weapons in South Korea. This spiked international concern about nuclear proliferation and resulted in negotiations after which, in 1985, Kim Il-Sung agreed to have North Korea sign onto the NPT. In 1991, the United States agreed to remove nuclear weapons from South Korea and, the following year, North and South Korea jointly agreed to denuclearize the entire peninsula and only to use nuclear technology for peaceful purposes. However, in 1993, the North Korean government rejected attempts by IAEA inspectors to enter the country and announced that the nation would pull out of the NPT. A series of negotiations with US representatives temporarily defused the situation, with North Korea agreeing to IAEA inspections in March of 1994. That same year, President Jimmy Carter met with Kim Il-Sung, resulting in an agreement in which North Korea agreed to completely eliminate their nuclear program in return for economic aid.[4]

After it was discovered that North Korea was continuing to develop its nuclear arsenal, US and DPRK representatives met for another series of talks in 1999, resulting in North Korea agreeing to suspend long-range missile tests and the United States easing economic sanctions against the DPRK for the first time since 1950. For a brief period in 2000, the United States, South Korea, and North Korea engaged in a series of diplomatic meetings, led by the Bill Clinton administration, with the goal of normalizing relations and preventing arms escalation. The United States eased sanctions further as meetings between North and South leaders appeared to mark a turning point and a potential normalization of relations.

While the Clinton administration was building towards a renewed nuclear agreement, the George W. Bush administration took a more antagonistic approach, insulting Kim Jong-Il and characterizing North Korea as part of a perceived "axis of evil," along with Iraq and Iran. In 2003, North Korea withdrew from the NPT completely and announced it would restart its nuclear weapons program.

A series of new negotiations between the United States, China, South Korea, Russia, Japan, and North Korea, called the "Six-Party Talks," failed to achieve substantive agreements, largely because both US and North Korean representatives refused to make any serious concessions. In 2005, between the first and second round of Six-Party Talks, the United States froze $25 million in North Korean funds being held in Banco Delta Asia, in Macao, which became a contentious issue in the ongoing effort to reach a renewed international agreement. At a further found of Six-Party Talks in 2005, North Korea agreed to abandon its nuclear program in return for economic assistance from the United States, Japan, Russia, and South Korea and the release of funds seized by the United States. Though the 2005 agreement put a system into place, there was no accepted framework for implementation and North Korea continued quietly developing its weapons technology.

In 2006, North Korea conducted the nation's first nuclear test, drawing international criticism and a new round of trade sanctions from the United Nations

Security Council. In February of that year, North Korea again agreed to suspend the program in return for a foreign aid package valued at nearly $400 million. However, discussions between the Bush administration and North Korea broke down over disagreements regarding the process to verify North Korea's compliance with shutting down its nuclear facilities. Diplomatic efforts began again under the Barack Obama administration in 2009, during which time North Korea continued engaging in missile tests. Talks failed when North Korea refused international inspections, resulting in new sanctions.[5]

The death of Kim Jong-Il, and his replacement by his son Kim Jong-Un, marked a new beginning for negotiations. Bilateral talks between Obama administration representatives and the Kim Jong-Un government resulted in a brief suspension of the nuclear program in 2012 in return for food aid from the United States after a severe famine left much of the North Korean population without food. However, North Korea's testing of a new intercontinental ballistic missile system in 2013 derailed peace talks. From 2013 to 2016, the Obama administration and allies opted to reinstate severe sanctions and utilize a strategy "strategic patience." Meanwhile, North Korea continued issuing announcements regarding new developments in the state's nuclear program. Analysis of these announcements differed, with some believing that North Korea was attempting to gain greater leverage in international negotiation and others believing that the United States should take more direct action to address the threat.

Egos and Big Buttons

The election of President Donald Trump signaled a new era in the US approach towards North Korea. Trump's initial approach was to issue a series of threats to the DPRK. For instance, on January 2, 2018, Trump tweeted:

> North Korean Leader Kim Jong Un just stated that the "Nuclear Button is on his desk at all times." Will someone from his depleted and food starved regime please inform him that I too have a Nuclear Button, but it is a much bigger & more powerful one than his, and my Button works![6]

Trump issued several other insulting statements through his Twitter account, referring to Kim Jong-Un as "rocket man." In response, Kim called Trump a "mentally deranged dotard." Donald Trump then insulted Kim's height and weight with this tweet, "Why would Kim Jong Un insult me by calling me 'old,' when I would NEVER call him 'short and fat'?" Kim responded by calling Trump a "rabid dog," at which point Trump tweeted, "North Korea best not make any more threats to the United States. They will be met with fire and fury like the world has never seen."[7]

Shortly thereafter, the Trump administration announced that they were changing tactics and beginning preparations for a historic summit meeting between Trump and Kim, the first time a North Korean leader and a US president had met in person since the Carter administration. The meeting was held in Singapore in June of 2018 and resulted in a joint agreement, signed by both leaders, claiming that they would both work toward complete nuclear disarmament of the entire Korean peninsula.

Though the Trump administration celebrated the meeting as a success, analysts were less sanguine.Since June, negotiations between Washington and North Korea appear to have stalled. The joint agreement did not include a timelineor any specific actions to be taken by either nation. In December of 2018, North Korea issued a statement claiming that the nation would not agree to disarmament until the United States agreed to end its "nuclear threat." Further statements from North Korea indicated also that continued US sanctions were another impediment to a more specific disarmament agreement. Moving into 2019, it remains unclear whether or not further meetings between Kim and Trump will materialize.

Sticking Points

North Korea's December 2018 announcement that the nation would not denuclearize until the United States agreed to make substantive agreements on sanctions and to end its "nuclear threat" indicate the primary obstacles to achieving North Korean disarmament. According to the Council on Foreign Relations (CFR), the United States and the United Nations Security Council (UNSC) have adopted the following economic sanctions and official condemnations toward North Korea:

October 14, 2006—Resolution 1718 sanctions against supply of missile technology, material, some luxury goods, and heavy weaponry.

June 12, 2009—Resolution 1874, strengthens above sanctions.

January 22, 2013—Resolution 2087 condemnation of satellite launch and other proliferation activities.

March 2, 2016—Resolution 2270 expands sanctions including banning member states from supplying aviation fuel to the DPRK.

November 30, 2016—Resolution 2321 expanded sanctions after nuclear test to include a ban on mineral exports such as copper and nickel, or selling statues and helicopters.

August 5, 2017—Resolution 2371 bans coal and iron exports.

December 22, 2017—Resolution 2397 bans oil imports and places sanctions on metal, agricultural, and labor exports.

In addition to UNSC sanctions, the United States has levied its own unilateral sanctions on North Korea in response to nuclear tests and development, human rights violations, and cyberattacks directed at the United States by state-sponsored Korean hackers. The United States has also placed sanctions on several Chinese and Russian firms accused of supporting North Korea. Most recently, in September of 2017, the United States issued a statement warning that any foreign financial institution that does business with North Korea can no longer do business with the United States. As of November of 2017, North Korea has been renamed as a "state sponsor of terrorism," despite being removed from that list by George W. Bush as part of his negotiation strategy.[8]

While nearly every administration has, in one way or another, either increased or eased sanctions as part of the ongoing negotiation process with North Korea, economic sanctions have had limited impact. Despite widespread poverty, food shortages, famine, and general economic hardship, the North Korean government has proven unwilling to submit to international demands on the basis of easing economic sanctions alone. However, the DPRK has demanded alterations to sanctions as its own requirement for negotiation and has repeatedly utilized the existence of ongoing sanctions as justification for failing to comply with disarmament agreements.

Finally, North Korea claims that the United States continues to pose a "nuclear threat" to their country. North Korea's state-run news agency, KCNA, explained its position with the statement:

> When we refer to the Korean peninsula, they include both the area of the DPRK and the area of south Korea where aggression troops including the nuclear weapons of the U.S. are deployed. When we refer to the denuclearization of the Korean peninsula, it therefore means removing all elements of nuclear threats from the areas of both the north and the south of Korea and also from surrounding areas from where the Korean peninsula is targeted.

Though the United States removed nuclear weapons from South Korea in 1991, it still maintains bombers and submarines in Japan and South Korea that could be used to attack North Korea. North Korea accuses the Trump administration of claiming to support denuclearization of the entire peninsula and calling for unilateral denuclearization of North Korea without removing military forces from locations that would be used to strike North Korea in the event of the war. The United States claims that it will not relieve sanctions unless North Korea begins disarming first and there is no mention of any effort to demilitarize Japan and South Korea in return for North Korean denuclearization.[9]

Even as talks between the United States and North Korea appear to have stalled, diplomatic connections between North and South Korea improved markedly over the past year, though the ultimate impact of this remains unclear. Some national security analysts have expressed hope that the softening of relations between the North and South may signal hope for disarmament or even for the Kim regime to bring North Korea more in line with the international community. As of 2019, the significance of this moment in the history of US-North Korean relations is unknown and it is likely that only after more time has passed, most likely overlapping into the next presidential administration, that the ultimate impact of the Trump administration's efforts with North Korea can be effectively evaluated.

Works Used

Albert, Eleanor. "What to Know About the Sanctions on North Korea." *CFR*. Council on Foreign Relations. Jan 3, 2018. Retrieved from https://www.cfr.org/backgrounder/what-know-about-sanctions-north-korea.

"Cold War." *GWU*. Eleanor Roosevelt Papers Project. George Washington University. 2015. Retrieved from https://www2.gwu.edu/~erpapers/teachinger/glossary/cold-war.cfm.

Gambino, Lauren. "Donald Trump Boasts That His Nuclear Button Is Bigger Than Kim Jong-un's." *The Guardian*. The Guardian News and Media. Jan 3, 2018.

Retrieved from https://www.theguardian.com/us-news/2018/jan/03/donald-trump-boasts-nuclear-button-bigger-kim-jong-un.

"Here's the Transcript of Trump's Press Conference After Meeting Kim Jong Un." *Market Watch.* MarketWatch Inc. June 12, 2018. Retrieved from https://www.marketwatch.com/story/heres-the-transcript-of-trumps-press-conference-after-meeting-kim-jong-un-2018-06-12.

Kim, Jeongmin and Josh Smith. "North Korea Media Says Denuclearization Includes Ending 'U.S. Nuclear Threat.'" *Reuters.* Reuters News Agency. Dec 20, 2018. Retrieved from https://www.reuters.com/article/us-northkorea-usa-denuclearisation/north-korea-media-says-denuclearization-includes-ending-u-s-nuclear-threat-idUSKCN1OJ0J1.

Kim, Min-Joo. "North Korea Rejects Denuclearization Unless U.S. 'Nuclear Threat' Is Eliminated." *The Washington Post.* The Washington Post Co. Dec 20, 2018. Retrieved from https://www.washingtonpost.com/world/asia_pacific/north-korea-rejects-denuclearization-unless-us-nuclear-threat-is-eliminated/2018/12/20/fc-f642a2-0438-11e9-b5df-5d3874f1ac36_story.html?utm_term=.2627043ee426.

"North Korean Nuclear Negotiations, 1985-2018." *CFR.* Council on Foreign Relations. 2018. Retrieved from https://www.cfr.org/timeline/north-korean-nuclear-negotiations.

"North Korea Nuclear Timeline Fast Facts." *CNN.* CNN. Apr 3, 2018. Retrieved from https://www.cnn.com/2013/10/29/world/asia/north-korea-nuclear-timeline---fast-facts/index.html.

"The Nuclear Non-Proliferation Treaty (NPT), 1968." *U.S. Department of State.* Office of the Historian. 2016. Retrieved from https://history.state.gov/milestones/1961-1968/npt.

"Singapore Mud-Sling: Donald Trump vs. Kim Jong Un Insults." *NDTV.* NDTV. Jun 11, 2018. Retrieved from https://www.ndtv.com/world-news/singapore-mud-sling-trump-vs-kim-insults-1865752.

Notes

1. "Here's the Transcript of Trump's Press Conference After Meeting Kim Jong Un," *Market Watch.*
2. Kim, "North Korea Rejects Denuclearization Unless U.S. 'Nuclear Threat' Is Eliminated."
3. "The Nuclear Non-Proliferation Treaty (NPT), 1968," *U.S. Department of State.*
4. "North Korean Nuclear Negotiations, 1985-2018," *CFR.*
5. "North Korea Nuclear Timeline Fast Facts," *CNN.*
6. Gambino, "Donald Trump Boasts That His Nuclear Button Is Bigger Than Kim Jong-un's."
7. "Singapore Mud-Sling: Donald Trump vs. Kim Jong Un Insults," *NDTV.*
8. Albert, "What to Know About the Sanctions on North Korea."
9. Kim and Smith, "North Korea Media Says Denuclearization Includes Ending 'U.S. Nuclear Threat.'"

Opinion: The U.S. and North Korea Have Made Progress. Here's How They Can Keep It Up

By Joel Wit
NPR, July 27, 2018

While the press has been full of stories about frustration with North Korea's lack of rapid follow-through on its denuclearization pledge at the Singapore summit, President Trump and Secretary of State Mike Pompeo are right in saying that the United States needs to give that process time.

North Korea recently began the apparent dismantling of key facilities at its Sohae space launch center, which is a step in the right direction, since they might be used to test ballistic missiles. So is Pyongyang's return of possible remains of American soldiers killed in the Korean War intended to help improve the political atmosphere for further talks.

But there is a long road ahead. And despite the political momentum created by the summit, there remains a danger that the effort will stall without steady progress.

Constant public sniping about the summit and its aftermath has obscured the positive steps taken by Washington, Seoul and Pyongyang over the past few months. No one would have predicted at the beginning of 2018 all the progress there has been to date—especially the U.S.-North Korean summit and the North's halting of missile and nuclear tests, the dismantlement of the nuclear test site and the apparent start of dismantlement of a major missile test facility—and now the return of possible remains of U.S. soldiers. Indeed, at the beginning of the year, most experts were asserting that the change in Kim Jong Un's line toward engagement was just another meaningless peace offensive.

Critics are right in asserting that, so far, none of these tangible measures touch on the core challenges of denuclearization—finally ridding Pyongyang of its nuclear weapons and the missiles to deliver them. However, dismissing them as mere window dressing is a mistake. Though limited, they are not meaningless in terms of their impact on North Korea's ability to modernize its nuclear and missile forces. These steps are important to build confidence and provide space for what are likely to be complicated negotiations to deal with central security concerns on both sides.

Washington now needs to take the denuclearization bull by the horns, first by recognizing that the United States has leverage over North Korea, not solely because of international sanctions, but also because of Kim's major focus on reforming his nation's economy. To do that, the North understands it needs, if not close, then at least less hostile, relations with the United States. And that, in turn, means ending what the North Koreans call the U.S. "hostile policy," including its constant emphasis, both in private and public, on ending the Korean War halted only by the temporary armistice that has been in place for 65 years.

In 2016, as North Korea escalated its nuclear and missile tests, I and a group of former U.S. government officials met overseas with North Korean government officials at a time when they seemed to be demanding negotiations to reach a peace treaty before talking about denuclearization. We were concerned that position was a trap since peace talks could drag on for years, delaying any hope of ending the nuclear threat. In fact, the North Koreans had in mind a parallel process, kicked off by a trilateral declaration by the U.S., North Korea and South Korea that the era of the war was over.

That is also the North Korean position today, highlighted by the Singapore summit declaration in June that pledges to establish "new U.S.-DPRK relations" and to "build a lasting and stable peace on the Korean Peninsula."

North Korea's Foreign Ministry issued a statement after Secretary of State Pompeo visited Pyongyang in early July. While the Western media fixated on a line that talked about America's "gangster-like demand," in fact the statement sent much the same message as the Singapore declaration.

Some experts continue to warn that we could get bogged down in peace talks and never have serious nuclear talks. But rather than viewing the North Korean position as a trap, the Trump administration should see it as positive leverage to secure its denuclearization objectives, starting with the following steps:

Secure information on Pyongyang's nuclear and missile programs: Since there are still uncertainties about North Korea's effort, a declaration will be essential. While the United States could try to secure a complete declaration right away, our judgment is that will prove to be a bridge too far, given years of tense relations. A more limited but significant initial step forward would be for the North to come clean on where it produces the nuclear material to build bombs—we

> **The North understands it needs, if not close, then at least less hostile, relations with the United States.**

may not be sure about some hidden plants—and how much material it has produced. Both will provide a firm basis for subsequent steps to verifiably freeze, roll back and eliminate its nuclear arsenal.

The Trump administration should also pick up on hints in the same Foreign Ministry statement about the North's willingness to curb the production of ballistic missiles by asking for information on where those missiles are assembled and how many have already been built. Again, these steps would be logical building blocks for further restrictions.

Build cooperation for on-site verification: In 1998, I led a team of Americans to inspect a North Korean military base near the Chinese border where the U.S. suspected Pyongyang was housing an underground nuclear reactor in violation of a denuclearization accord with the United States. The inspection, which found that there was no underground reactor, worked because of North Korean cooperation built on improving political relations between the two countries.

Today, however, after years of hostility, rather than seeking highly intrusive inspections right off the bat, it might be wise to first work out cooperation-building measures. For example, the North could allow foreign inspectors to visit its nuclear test site and other facilities Pyongyang has been dismantling to confirm its claims.

Get the denuclearization ball rolling: Since it isn't going to happen overnight, the U.S. and North Korea need to start work on a negotiated, phased agreement that directly affects the North's ability to produce weapons.

For example, North Korea could convert the Yongbyon nuclear facility—where it produces fissile materials indispensible in building nuclear weapons—to a scientific and industrial park engaged in helping to modernize the North Korean economy. That would require an immediate suspension of all activities at the site to be observed by foreign inspectors, a permanent end to those activities by disabling and dismantling key facilities and moving to establish new ones that could gainfully employ the thousands of engineers, technicians and workers at Yongbyon previously engaged in building weapons. One possibility is the production of radioisotopes used in nuclear medicine that are in short global supply.

Any new agreement should also include the dismantlement of all remaining rocket engine test sites in North Korea that could be used to develop long-range missiles.

All of these steps would present important progress, but they can't be achieved without hard work and, most importantly, a serious negotiating effort. That hard work cannot be done by Pompeo during two-day visits to Pyongyang or a U.S.-North Korean "working group" that meets at the Demilitarized Zone that divides the two Koreas. It will require a sustained, face-to-face effort that may take weeks, and probably months.

Quickly appointing a special representative to lead talks with the North is a step in the right direction. But that will not be enough, given the enormous task ahead. Secretary Pompeo will have to remain closely involved, perhaps participating in talks at key junctures to resolve tough issues. And so will President Trump through more summits with Kim Jong Un.

Print Citations

CMS: Wit, Joel. "Opinion: The U.S. and North Korea Have Made Progress. Here's How They Can Keep It Up." In *The Reference Shelf: The Two Koreas*, edited by Micah L. Issit, 95-98. Ipswich, MA: H.W. Wilson, 2019.

MLA: Wit, Joel. "Opinion: The U.S. and North Korea Have Made Progress. Here's How They Can Keep It Up." *The Reference Shelf: The Two Koreas,* edited by Micah L. Issit, H.W. Wilson, 2019, pp. 95-98.

APA: Wit, J. (2019). Opinion: The U.S. and North Korea have made progress. Here's how they can keep it up. In Micah L. Issit (Ed.), *The reference shelf: The two Koreas* (pp. 95-98). Ipswich, MA: H.W. Wilson.

South Korea Reveals Plan to Break Stalemate in U.S.–North Korea Talks

By John Hudson

The Washington Post, October 3, 2018

South Korea is proposing that the United States hold off on a demand for an inventory of North Korea's nuclear weapons and accept the verified closure of a key North Korean nuclear facility as a next step in the negotiations, Seoul's top diplomat said in an interview with the *Washington Post*.

The plan is designed to break the impasse between North Korea and the United States as President Trump comes under mounting pressure to demonstrate progress on the denuclearization talks. It will be one of the options available to Secretary of State Mike Pompeo as he arrives in North Korea on Sunday to restart negotiations.

In exchange for the verified dismantlement of the Yongbyon nuclear facility, the United States would declare an end to the Korean War, a key demand of Pyongyang that U.S. officials have been reluctant to make absent a major concession by North Korea.

"What North Korea has indicated is they will permanently dismantle their nuclear facilities in Yongbyon, which is a very big part of their nuclear program," South Korean Foreign Minister Kang Kyung-wha said during a discussion at the South Korean mission to the United Nations. "If they do that in return for America's corresponding measures, such as the end-of-war declaration, I think that's a huge step forward for denuclearization."

Sustained fighting in the Korean War ended with a truce in 1953, but a formal peace treaty has never been signed. In recent weeks, North Korea has demanded almost daily that the United States sign an end-of-war declaration.

U.S. negotiators have tried to get North Korea to provide a list of nuclear facilities and weapons they want dismantled but failed to secure an agreement even after Trump's meeting with North Korean leader Kim Jong Un in Singapore and three trips to North Korea by Pompeo.

On Tuesday, North Korea's state-run broadcaster again called the demands for a nuclear inventory "rubbish."

Kang said demanding a list at the outset risks bogging down the negotiations in a subsequent dispute over verification. As an example, she cited the deterioration of negotiations between North Korea and the George W. Bush administration after Pyongyang handed over thousands of pages of documents on its main plutonium-related facilities in 2008.

"The past experience shows that the list and the verification about the list takes a lot of back-and-forth, and I think the last time things broke down precisely as we were working out a detailed protocol on verification after we had gotten the list ... We want to take a different approach," she said.

Stressing the importance of stopping the further production of nuclear materials at the Yongbyon facility, she added: "We will have to see an inventory at some point, but that some point can be reached more expeditiously by action and corresponding measures that give the two sides sufficient trust."

Whether Seoul can persuade Washington to take up the proposed bargain remains to be seen. The State Department declined to comment on its willingness to delay demands for an inventory or declare an end to the Korean War.

Hawks inside the Trump administration, in particular national security adviser John Bolton, remain skeptical of signing such a declaration out of fear that it will give North Korea and China justification to demand the removal of the 28,500 U.S. forces stationed in South Korea, people close to Bolton said, speaking on the condition of anonymity to discuss the sensitive negotiations.

Kang downplayed concerns about the declaration, emphasizing that it would be a purely "political" document and "not a legally binding treaty."

Trump, according to diplomats familiar with the negotiations, is open to signing the declaration and may not be bothered by ensuing demands about U.S. forces given his long-standing complaint that the United States pays far too much to station troops in East Asia.

Analysts briefed on South Korea's proposal offered mixed assessments.

"If the Yongbyon shutdown proves to be the first bite of the apple, it might be an okay starting point, but if it proves to be the only bite of the apple, it will be deeply unsatisfying—and totally reversible," said Scott Snyder, a Korea expert at the Council on Foreign Relations.

Duyeon Kim, a Korea expert with the Center for a New American Security, said the closure of Yongbyon would be a "welcome" and "tangible" step but noted that North Korea would still be able to expand its nuclear arsenal and fissile material production at covert facilities elsewhere in the country.

"It's unrealistic to expect a comprehensive, completely accurate list from the get-go, but the administration should still insist that Pyongyang at least disclose all fuel-cycle-related facilities anywhere in the country," she said

On Tuesday, State Department spokeswoman Heather Nauert said Pompeo would arrive in North Korea on Sunday but gave few details about the status of the negotiations. "Obviously these conversations are going in the right direction and we feel confident enough to hop on a plane to head there to continue the conversations," she said.

The U.S. outlook on the negotiations has been difficult to surmise as Trump hails major accomplishments going on behind closed doors, while Pyongyang falls short of key U.S. demands, including providing its understanding of denuclearization and the number of weapons and amount of bomb fuel it has.

"If you saw what's going on behind the scenes, I think you'd be very impressed," Trump said last week. "I've received two letters from Chairman Kim … They're letters that are magnificent in the sense of his feeling for wanting to get this done."

North Korea has already signaled that it may drive a hard bargain during Pompeo's fourth visit. Despite calling for the end-of-war declaration, the Korean Central News Agency said Tuesday that the document "can never be a bargaining chip for getting the DPRK denuclearized" and that the United States must ease economic sanctions before North Korea takes steps.

"If the U.S. doesn't want the end of war, the DPRK will also not particularly hope for it," the news agency said in a commentary.

The North has also given Pompeo's new special representative for North Korea, Stephen Biegun, the cold shoulder, said U.S. officials, who also spoke on the condition of anonymity to discuss the sensitive talks. Last month, Pompeo publicly invited Pyongyang to meet with Biegun in Vienna at the "earliest opportunity," but the request went unanswered and the North has yet to name a counterpart for Biegun, they said.

Kang, South Korea's first female foreign minister, is trying to build momentum behind the U.S.-North Korea talks despite international skepticism that Kim is willing to surrender his nuclear arsenal.

In the process, she and South Korean President Moon Jae-in have fended off allegations of naivete from Japanese and American counterparts who say their belief in dialogue blinds them to Kim's deceptive nature.

Kang said her government has no illusions about the nature of the Kim dynasty, a fact that guides her thinking on negotiating tactics.

"We know North Korea better than any party in this process," she said. "We are as keen and perhaps as committed as anybody on getting to complete denuclearization … Naivete is certainly not something that would characterize my government's approach to North Korea."

Moon, a former human rights lawyer, and Kang, a former U.N. deputy high commissioner for human rights, have both come under pressure to underscore human rights violations in North Korea, which is accused of incarcerating tens of thousands of citizens in labor camps dedicated to political crimes among many other abuses.

Kang said Seoul supports efforts by the international community to advance human rights in North Korea but acknowledged that denuclearization is the most paramount concern for her country.

"The North Korean human rights situation is a global issue, and we are part of the global discussions," she said. "There are times to raise these issues. Certainly not at this time, when we very much need to move forward on the denuclearization issue."

Trump, whose advisers initially sought a quick deal with North Korea, told reporters last week he's in no "rush."

Kang said the remarks reflect the complexity of the negotiations. "I think there is a lot more understanding and appreciation of the difficulty of the issue," she said. "This is a very advanced program, so you can't just dismantle it or do away with it in a matter of a short period."

Print Citations

CMS: Hudson, John. "South Korea Reveals Plan to Break Stalemate in U.S.—North Korea Talks." In *The Reference Shelf: The Two Koreas*, edited by Micah L. Issit, 99-102. Ipswich, MA: H.W. Wilson, 2019.

MLA: Hudson, John. "South Korea Reveals Plan to Break Stalemate in U.S.—North Korea Talks. *The Reference Shelf: The Two Koreas*, edited by Micah L. Issit, H.W. Wilson, 2019, pp. 99-102.

APA: Hudson, J. (2019). South Korea reveals plan to break stalemate in U.S.—North Korea talks. In Micah L. Issit (Ed.), *The reference shelf: The two Koreas* (pp. 99-102). Ipswich, MA: H.W. Wilson.

U.S. Has Little To Show for Stalled Nuclear Talks with North Korea

By Tracy Wilkinson and Victoria Kim
Los Angeles Times, November 22, 2018

Nearly six months after President Trump and North Korean leader Kim Jong Un embraced at a historic Singapore summit and made vague promises of peace and prosperity, talks have flatlined and Pyongyang has taken no significant steps to reduce its nuclear arsenal or production facilities.

Fears of all-out war clearly have eased in Northeast Asia since the two leaders stopped trading crude insults and invective, as they had in the months before the June 12 summit. And U.S. officials point to confidence-building measures, including North Korea's suspension since last spring of additional nuclear weapons and ballistic missile tests.

But denuclearization, the primary U.S. goal, appears as distant as ever, analysts and diplomats say. The on-again, off-again diplomatic process appears to have foundered and experts say North Korea is secretly expanding its nuclear and missile capabilities, just as it has during previous U.S. attempts to negotiate with the regime since the mid-1990s.

In the latest dust-up, on Nov. 7, North Korean officials abruptly called off a planned meeting in New York with Secretary of State Michael R. Pompeo and threatened to resume nuclear testing unless the Trump administration lifts sanctions. Working-level meetings also have ground to a halt, State Department officials said.

Kim may prefer to wait for a second summit with Trump, who told the United Nations on Sept. 24 that he would meet with the North Korean leader again "very soon." The White House has not announced a date or location for that meeting.

The North Koreans "don't want to deal with bureaucrats. They think they can get the best deal possible" directly from Trump, said Sue Mi Terry, a former CIA analyst specializing in the Korean peninsula who now is at the Center for Strategic and International Studies, a nonpartisan think tank in Washington.

Pyongyang has stepped up pressure in other ways. The state-run news agency reported this month that Kim personally oversaw the testing of what it called an "ultra-modern," cutting-edge tactical weapon that took seven years to develop. The news agency provided no details of the alleged weapon.

More significantly, in August, the International Atomic Energy Agency reported that North Korea was taking action consistent with enrichment of uranium and construction at its main nuclear site. The U.N. nuclear watchdog agency called the "further development" of the nuclear program "a cause for grave concern."

A separate think tank report warned that commercial satellite photos had revealed 13 missile development bases that it said North Korea had concealed. Pyongyang had never agreed to dismantle infrastructure for its ballistic missiles, and the White House said that U.S. intelligence already knew about the sites.

Still, in building up its missile facilities, North Korea is "raising the price" on any potential deal with the U.S. by expanding the list of items it could use to demand concessions from the Trump administration, said Bruce Klingner, a former CIA deputy division chief for Korea who is now a senior research fellow at the Heritage Foundation, a conservative think tank in Washington.

"You don't build them up to turn around and abandon them," he said of the sites.

Adding to the challenge, U.S. officials say, is that China has eased up its enforcement of U.N. economic sanctions on North Korea since the Singapore summit—in part a reflection of Trump's acrimonious relations with Beijing. China is North Korea's largest trading partner, and Kim has repeatedly met with Chinese President Xi Jinping this year.

North Korea has balked at handing over a detailed inventory of its nuclear arsenal and production facilities, a key U.S. demand, saying its enemies would simply use it as a targeting list. IAEA inspectors would require a detailed inventory to inspect and confirm any claims of denuclearization.

Vice President Mike Pence recently said the U.S. goal in a second summit would be to develop a plan for a nuclear inventory and international inspections as a starting point for ultimately dismantling North Korea's nuclear weapons.

"I think it will be absolutely imperative in this next summit that we come away with a plan for identifying all of the weapons in question, identifying all the development sites, allowing for inspections of the sites, and the plan for dismantling nuclear weapons," Pence told *NBC News* on Nov. 15.

Less clear is what concessions Trump may offer or agree to if a summit occurs. In addition to the lifting of U.S. sanctions, Kim wants a formal end to the Korean War, the early Cold War conflict that saw a U.S.-led U.N. force battle communist North Korea and its Chinese backers into a stalemate. Fighting was suspended in 1953 but the war never officially ended, and the Korean peninsula has been divided ever since.

Experts say North Korea is secretly expanding its nuclear and missile capabilities, just as it has during previous U.S. attempts to negotiate with the regime since the mid-1990s.

The Pentagon keeps about 28,000 troops in South Korea. Ending the war could increase pressure to withdraw those forces, and jeopardize the American military and diplomatic alliance with Seoul, one of the United States' closest allies.

South Korean President Moon Jae-in has been a cheerleader for detente with North Korea. That's raised concerns in Washington that in his eagerness to improve relations between the Koreas, Moon may allow Pyongyang to drive a wedge between the U.S. and South Korea. Washington is especially worried that Seoul may ease up on sanctions targeting the North.

South Korea's unification minister, Cho Myoung-gyon, sought to allay those fears in a recent address at the Wilson Center think tank in Washington. He said South Korea has emphasized cultural exchanges and family reunifications, but economic sanctions would remain as long as the nuclear threat exists.

"Korea and the U.S. [are] on the same page to achieve the same goal," Cho said.

Officials in Seoul said long-broken railway lines between the North and South should be reconnected by year's end. A South Korean envoy told reporters that the Trump administration gave its blessing to the project. Cho said Kim may visit Seoul within the year as well, continuing a series of meetings he's had with Moon.

Publicly, the Trump administration has remained optimistic about its dealings with North Korea and defended its pursuit of denuclearization.

Pompeo said on Oct. 7, after a visit to Pyongyang, that Kim had agreed to allow U.N. inspectors into the country to inspect the Punggye-ri nuclear test site, which North Korea claims it destroyed in May by blowing up several tunnels. No inspections have taken place.

"As soon as we get it logistically worked out, Chairman Kim said he's ready to allow them to come in," Pompeo said at the time. "There's a lot of logistics that will be required to execute that."

Heather Nauert, a State Department spokeswoman, said that administration officials "go into this with our eyes wide open" and that although there is "work that's left to be done," progress has been made.

"A lot of people like to pooh-pooh that idea," she said. But, she added, "we have still come a long way from where we were in our relationship and our posture with North Korea in the past year. We see that as progress."

Print Citations

CMS: Wilkinson, Tracy, and Victoria Kim. "U.S. Has Little to Show for Stalled Nuclear Talks with North Korea." In *The Reference Shelf: The Two Koreas*, edited by Micah L. Issit, 103-105. Ipswich, MA: H.W. Wilson, 2019.

MLA: Wilkinson, Tracy, and Victoria Kim. "U.S. Has Little to Show for Stalled Nuclear Talks with North Korea." *The Reference Shelf: The Two Koreas,* edited by Micah L. Issit, H.W. Wilson, 2019, pp. 103-105.

APA: Wilkinson, T., & Kim, V. (2019). U.S. has little to show for stalled nuclear talks with North Korea. In Micah L. Issit (Ed.), *The reference shelf: The two Koreas* (pp. 103-105). Ipswich, MA: H.W. Wilson.

Why There Has Been No Progress in Nuclear Talks with North Korea

By L.R.S.

The Economist, November 19, 2018

"There is no longer a Nuclear Threat from North Korea," President Donald Trump tweeted in June. Mr Trump had just returned from a meeting in Singapore with Kim Jong Un, North Korea's dictator. During the meeting, he claimed, Mr Kim had agreed to give up his nuclear programme in return for American security guarantees and, eventually, relief from sanctions. But more than five months later, the nuclear threat is alive and well. Intelligence reports suggest that Mr Kim is expanding his programme rather than rolling it back. On November 16th North Korea reported that the army had successfully tested an unspecified "ultramodern tactical weapon", the first public reference to a recent weapons test since November 2017. So why have things hit a snag?

On the face of it, the process turns on differing interpretations of what Mr Kim actually pledged to do. In the text signed in June, the two countries agree to "establish new US-DPRK relations" and "build a lasting and stable peace regime" while North Korea "commits to work toward complete denuclearisation of the Korean Peninsula." America has since insisted that any concessions it offers must be preceded by clear Korean moves towards denuclearisation, such as handing over a complete list of nuclear facilities and allowing inspections of sites that have allegedly been dismantled. But apart from a freeze on nuclear tests (which actually preceded the Singapore summit), North Korea has only offered symbolic gestures, like publicly blowing up a test site it no longer needed. Before taking more concrete steps, it is demanding that America reciprocate, for instance by lifting some sanctions. Follow-up talks have not succeeded in bridging the gap. Earlier this month, a meeting between Mike Pompeo, America's secretary of state, and Kim Yong Chol, the North's chief negotiator, was cancelled by the North at the last minute.

Mr Kim may be prepared to give up his nuclear weapons, and may simply want more tangible guarantees before he starts the process. But it is more likely that he wants to hang on to the nukes, which the regime has pursued for decades to ensure its survival, and is using the current round of negotiations to try to extract concessions from America. After all, the North has a history of making other countries pay for promises on which it then reneges. Mr Trump's relentless overselling of the deal reached in Singapore, which contains no details of how the denuclearisation is meant to come about, has encouraged such behaviour. Mr Kim is exploiting the vagueness of his own promises to stall the process, all the while accusing America of bad faith.

> **The North has a history of making other countries pay for promises on which it then reneges.**

For now, the process remains in a rut. No serious arms-control agreement is possible unless Mr Kim hands over a list of his nuclear facilities, but there is no sign that he will do this. Indeed, the North's state media has recently ramped up its rhetoric again, threatening to return to nuclear testing unless America makes the concessions that Mr Kim claims it promised. In response, America has vowed to keep up sanctions and pressure on the regime. But it has also made emollient noises. On November 15th Mike Pence, the vice-president, said that a second meeting between Mr Trump and Mr Kim may go ahead without North Korea having to show the much-discussed nuclear-facilities list. America's adoption of the North's view of denuclearisation may ensure that talks continue, defusing the risk of re-escalation. But it is unlikely to bring an end to the North's nuclear programme.

Print Citations

CMS: "Why There Has Been No Progress in Nuclear Talks with North Korea." In *The Reference Shelf: The Two Koreas,* edited by Micah L. Issit, 106-107. Ipswich, MA: H.W. Wilson, 2019.

MLA: "Why There Has Been No Progress in Nuclear Talks with North Korea." *The Reference Shelf: The Two Koreas,* edited by Micah L. Issit, H.W. Wilson, 2019, pp. 106-107.

APA: The Economist. (2019). Why there has been no progress in nuclear talks with North Korea. In Micah L. Issit (Ed.), *The reference shelf: The two Koreas* (pp. 106-107). Ipswich, MA: H.W. Wilson.

North Korea Accuses Washington of Weaponizing Human Rights as Nuclear Talks Stall

By Choe Sang-Hun
The New York Times, November 29, 2018

SEOUL, South Korea—North Korea has lashed out at the United States for continuing to press it to improve its human rights record, even with animosities between the two countries having eased so much that President Trump said he and the North's leader, Kim Jong-un, were "in love."

North Korean diplomats and the state news media have unleashed blistering attacks on Washington since the United Nations' human rights committee adopted a resolution this month condemning North Korea's "longstanding and ongoing systematic, widespread and gross violations of human rights." The resolution, similar versions of which have been adopted each year since 2005, is certain to be approved by the 193-member United Nations General Assembly next month.

As it did following the past resolutions, Washington is calling a United Nations Security Council meeting early next month to discuss human rights in North Korea and inviting the United Nations' top human rights official, Michelle Bachelet, to address the session.

North Korea has invariably denounced such resolutions as attempts to overthrow its political system. But this year, it said the human rights "racket" raised by American diplomats at the United Nations was poisoning the mood for talks on denuclearizing North Korea following the historic summit meeting between Mr. Kim and Mr. Trump in Singapore in June.

At the Singapore meeting, Mr. Kim offered a vague promise to "work toward the complete denuclearization of the Korean Peninsula." But talks have since stalled, with Washington demanding a full declaration of the North's nuclear assets for future inspections and the North insisting that Washington first lift sanctions before it takes steps toward denuclearizing.

"Thanks to the peace-loving efforts of the D.P.R.K., the atmosphere of peace and stability has recently settled down in the Korean Peninsula," Kim Song, the North Korean ambassador to the United Nations, said in a letter to Security Council members, using the acronym of his country's official name, Democratic People's Republic of Korea.

The letter accused the Council of seeking to "stoke confrontation, instead of encouraging and promoting the ongoing positive developments" of talks between the United States and the North.

In the letter, first obtained by the *Associated Press* this week, Mr. Kim urged Council members to vote against convening a meeting.

The North's state-run newspaper, Rodong Sinmun, carried a similarly strident commentary on the issue on Monday, denying there were any human rights abuses in the North.

"The reason that the Americans are so obsessed with this absurdity is that they want to sully the image of our republic in order to justify their racket for sanctions and pressure and to extract our concessions in their negotiations with us," it said.

Concerns about human rights abuses in North Korea have long undermined relations between Pyongyang and Washington.

Over the years, the United Nations and international human rights groups have published numerous reports on the problem, including a 2014 report by a United Nations commission concluding that human rights violations in North Korea amounted to crimes against humanity. In a report last month, Human Rights Watch ac-

> **The United States has vowed to continue raising concerns about human rights in North Korea, but it also says the priority is denuclearizing the country.**

cused prison guards and other officials in the North of rape and other sexual crimes against women.

In a speech at the South Korean Parliament last November, Mr. Trump made among the strongest criticisms of any American leader of "the horror of life in North Korea." He called the country a "cruel dictatorship" and said that "an estimated 100,000 North Koreans suffer in gulags, toiling in forced labor, and enduring torture, starvation, rape and murder on a constant basis."

Three weeks later, North Korea launched an intercontinental ballistic missile deemed powerful enough to reach the continental United States.

But Mr. Trump's tone has changed dramatically this year, especially after his meeting with Kim Jong-un in June.

"Well, he is very talented," Mr. Trump said of Mr. Kim shortly after meeting with him in Singapore. He said they had discussed human rights "relatively briefly compared to denuclearization."

The United States has vowed to continue raising concerns about human rights in North Korea, but it also says the priority is denuclearizing the country.

"Our Human Rights Report is very clear about the concerns that we have not just about North Korea but many countries, frankly, around the world and countries that can do a lot better," Heather Nauert, a State Department spokeswoman, said last month. "Our priority in North Korea, though, right now is denuclearization."

Print Citations

CMS: Choe, Sang-Hun. "North Korea Accuses Washington of Weaponizing Human Rights as Nuclear Talks Stall." In *The Reference Shelf: The Two Koreas,* edited by Micah L. Issit, 108-110. Ipswich, MA: H.W. Wilson, 2019.

MLA: Choe, Sang-Hun. "North Korea Accuses Washington of Weaponizing Human Rights as Nuclear Talks Stall." *The Reference Shelf: The Two Koreas,* edited by Micah L. Issit, H.W. Wilson, 2019, pp. 108-110.

APA: Choe, S.-H. (2019). North Korea accuses Washington of weaponizing human rights as nuclear talks stall. In Micah L. Issit (Ed.), *The reference shelf: The two Koreas* (pp. 108-110). Ipswich, MA: H.W. Wilson.

Can the U.S. Reinstate "Maximum Pressure" on North Korea?

By Eric Brewer

Foreign Affairs, December 4, 2018

The diplomatic sprint to North Korean denuclearization has slowed to a crawl. Earlier last month, North Korea abruptly canceled talks with U.S. Secretary of State Mike Pompeo, with reports suggesting that Pyongyang continues to enhance its nuclear and missile capabilities. Despite U.S. President Donald Trump's insistence that North Korean leader Kim Jong Un is serious about giving up his nuclear weapons, chances are good that the United States is going to need a Plan B to manage the nuclear threat.

Unfortunately, the air had already been leaking out of the Trump administration's "maximum pressure" strategy since early to mid-2018. Worse still, it will likely prove extremely difficult to revive international efforts to squeeze North Korea if the current diplomatic push hits a dead end. Key countries that were supportive of the pressure campaign—most notably China and South Korea—are intent on mending ties with Pyongyang, which for now has ceased the type of provocations that could unite the world against it. Meanwhile, Trump's lavish praise of Kim has further impeded the United States' ability to rally foreign partners to pressure the North.

If current trends continue, any attempt to reinstate maximum pressure may well prove ineffective. The hard collapse of diplomacy could dangerously narrow U.S. policy options and make military conflict more likely.

A Three-Pronged Strategy

The North Korea maximum-pressure strategy rested on three pillars that, as of early 2018, were effectively squeezing the North Korean regime. The first was a series of United Nations Security Council Resolutions in 2017 that banned North Korea's most lucrative exports, including coal, iron ore, seafood, and textiles. This meant that about 90 percent of North Korean exports—which stood to net the regime about $2.7 billion—were now illegal. These resolutions also reduced the North's most critical import—oil—and laid the legal foundations to cut off various North Korean workarounds, such as at-sea transfers of illicit cargo from one ship to another (known as "ship-to-ship" transfers). For the first time, world powers, including

China, had finally agreed to meaningfully target those things that mattered most to the regime: revenue and oil.

UN resolutions, however, are effective only if enforced. Accordingly, the United States engaged in intensive diplomatic outreach—the second pillar of the strategy—to encourage countries to clamp down on North Korean illicit activity. The Trump team made the pressure campaign a top priority. As a result, partners could be sure that at almost every diplomatic encounter, the United States would bring a number of concrete proposals to rein in North Korean behavior. Washington was willing to put other policies on the line in service of this strategy. For example, the U.S. withheld military aid to Egypt in 2017 in part because of the country's continued ties to North Korea.

This diplomatic strategy soon began to pay off. By September 2017, over 20 countries had restricted North Korea's diplomatic activities, which Pyongyang uses to aid its sanctions evasion. The United States was also able to keep South Korea aligned with the pressure campaign. Most important, Washington persuaded Beijing to up the pressure by more rigorously enforcing UN sanctions—which, in turn, put added strain on North Korea's economy and caused relations between China and North Korea to plummet.

The United States also expanded its own sanctions efforts against Pyongyang—the third pillar of the strategy. This included significantly upping the number and scope of sanctions designations and implementing a new executive order that made it easier to go after third parties such as banks and businesses that aided North Korean entities. These measures not only denied access to the U.S. financial system but also helped draw attention to problematic North Korean behaviors—such as Pyongyang's attempts to mask the origin of its ships and illicit cargo. By demonstrating increased willingness to impose economic costs on those who

What was a key enabler of U.S. successes in 2017—Chinese and South Korean cooperation—is now a vulnerability.

did business with North Korea—including China—the United States encouraged countries to distance themselves from Pyongyang to avoid becoming a target of U.S. sanctions.

In practice, these three efforts were complementary. The U.S. approach to combating North Korean attempts to illicitly acquire fuel through ship-to-ship transfers is instructive. Through a combination of UN bans on at-sea transfers, intelligence and diplomatic efforts that exposed North Korean tactics and pressured Pyongyang's enablers, and U.S. and UN sanctions on entities involved, the United States made significant headway against North Korean cheating. The goal was not to convince North Korea to stop evading sanctions or to prevent every illegal shipment—an impossible task—but to raise the costs of working with North Korea for other nations and third parties.

A Sudden Shift

The maximum-pressure strategy probably could not have forced North Korea to give up its entire nuclear weapons program. But it stood the best chance of providing the United States leverage to secure meaningful reductions and limits from Pyongyang. Exactly how well it could have worked will remain an unknown, because without warning Trump pivoted to premature diplomacy with Kim.

Trump's sudden announcement in March that he would accept Kim's invitation to meet opened the diplomatic relief valve on the pressure campaign. In the months that followed, Kim and South Korean President Moon Jae-in would have three diplomatic summits. Kim would also travel to China for three visits with President Xi Jinping, including Kim's first ever trip outside of North Korea and first meeting with a head of state since coming to power. As if flipping a switch, Trump shifted from issuing threats and personal insults against Kim to praising him as a "very honorable" leader.

Many elements of the pressure strategy still exist in theory and on paper. Sanctions remain in place, and the United States is working to enforce them. But the North Korean regime's high tolerance for economic pain and adeptness at evading sanctions mean that if Washington is not adding pressure on North Korea, it is losing pressure. Building and sustaining momentum is critical, especially if the goal is to force Kim to conclude he needs to make cuts to his arsenal to survive.

Unfortunately, the maximum-pressure campaign against North Korea has been losing momentum since early to mid-2018. Three developments are eroding the conditions that made it work. First, key partners—namely, China and South Korea—are easing up on pressure and are highly unlikely to jump back into an aggressive U.S. strategy just because Washington says so. Reports indicate that China has slackened in sanctions enforcement, including by relaxing inspections of goods flowing across the Chinese–North Korean border. Chinese leaders—along with Russian officials—are increasing calls for sanctions relief to aid diplomatic efforts. China clearly has no appetite for stronger measures at this juncture. Relations between Kim and Xi have rebounded since last year, and increasing economic and political tensions between the United States and China give Beijing even fewer reasons to cooperate.

The more dramatic shift is in South Korea, where Moon appears intent on forging ahead toward reconciling with Pyongyang and seems unwilling to let Washington's goal of denuclearization dictate the pace of the inter-Korean peace-building efforts. This is creating political tensions between Seoul and Washington—surely to Pyongyang's content. Thus, what was a key enabler of U.S. successes in 2017—Chinese and South Korean cooperation—is now a vulnerability. A U.S. decision to suddenly ramp up pressure would be fighting against the political headwinds in the region, and is unlikely to succeed.

Absent a resumption of North Korean nuclear or missile testing—or North Korea unilaterally walking away from talks—China and Russia are unlikely to back new UN Security Council resolutions. North Korea's missile and nuclear provocations in 2017—including its first ever ICBM test, missile launches over Japan, threats to strike Guam, and a claimed thermonuclear nuclear test—provided flashpoints that united the international community around tougher UN measures. The United States needs to entertain the possibility that Kim means at least some of what he says: that he's sufficiently satisfied with the results of his testing, and has moved his focus to mass production of nuclear weapons and missiles.

Most important, Trump's embrace of Kim and his continued insistence that the nuclear challenge is all but resolved have cut the legs out from under the U.S. pressure campaign. His advisers and those at the working level of North Korea policy are now at a disadvantage when it comes to trying to sustain pressure. True, Trump has stated that sanctions will remain in force until North Korea denuclearizes. But his general change in rhetoric—including his pronouncement that he no longer wants to use the term "maximum pressure" because the United States and North Korea are "getting along"—and apparent willful blindness to events on the ground speak louder. This provides other countries with top cover to resist or ignore U.S. entreaties on sanctions enforcement, and is being used by North Korea to avoid taking steps toward denuclearization.

Trump's shift in approach has affected U.S. pressure policy as well: the number of new U.S. sanctions designations has dropped dramatically—a decline of about 85 percent—since Trump's March decision to meet Kim, in comparison to the year prior when the pressure campaign was in full swing. (Although the administration admittedly still has a few months to catch up, it would need to drastically increase its pace of sanctions designations.) Curtailing further sanctions makes sense if one believes, as Trump apparently does, that Kim has already made the choice to give up his nuclear weapons. But if this round of diplomacy by Kim is just the North's latest bid to get sanctions relief and gain acceptance of its nuclear arsenal, such a slowdown works in his favor.

The Pressure's On

If the United States is to have any hope of resuming a serious pressure campaign, it needs to revamp its diplomatic process in such a way that it can return to maximum pressure should negotiations fail.

To begin, the administration should drop its maximalist demands that seek quick denuclearization and only promise sanctions relief when the last nuclear weapon has left North Korea. This plan stands almost no chance of being accepted by Pyongyang, and gives China, South Korea, and others the impression that the United States isn't seriously interested in finding a solution. That's bad for pressure, as the United States will be blamed if and when diplomacy fails. Instead, Washington should prioritize developing a roadmap with Pyongyang that lays out a step-by-step approach that provides rewards along the way commensurate with North Korean actions.

As part of this plan, the United States also needs to disabuse North Korea of the notion that it can avoid working-level dialogue while holding out for the one-on-one meeting with Trump, where Kim believes he's more likely to get what he wants. The United States should refuse a second summit unless such dialogue occurs and produces something for the two sides to agree on: in essence, no pageantry without a process.

U.S. diplomats then need to take this plan—which stands a better chance of success—on the road, making clear that diplomacy will only work if all are united in maintaining pressure on North Korea. They should also seek to negotiate new steps to increase pressure now in the event North Korea does not take advantage of this diplomatic window. The logic is clear: since Pyongyang has not stopped adding to its nuclear and missile arsenal—a violation of its commitments—there is no reason for the international community to throttle back its pressure.

Washington can also take unilateral steps now to prevent the further erosion of pressure in ways that are less likely to upset the diplomatic apple cart. For example, the administration should build on its wise decision announced last month to create a working group with South Korea on North Korea by pushing for a similar, but perhaps more narrowly focused, working group with Beijing. Washington could also expand sanctions designations against third parties involved in illicit North Korean activities.

Those who fear a return to the days of Trump's threats to "totally destroy" North Korea should support developing a smooth transition to greater international pressure if and when the time comes. After all, the failure to attract an international coalition is more likely to lead the Trump administration to rely on unilateral—and possibly military—measures. Taking these steps will preserve the option of returning to an effective maximum-pressure campaign, and will also make it more likely that Trump's diplomatic gambit succeeds.

Print Citations

CMS: Brewer, Eric. "Can the U.S. Reinstate 'Maximum Pressure' on North Korea?" In *The Reference Shelf: The Two Koreas,* edited by Micah L. Issit, 111-115. Ipswich, MA: H.W. Wilson, 2019.

MLA: Brewer, Eric. "Can the U.S. Reinstate 'Maximum Pressure' on North Korea?" *The Reference Shelf: The Two Koreas,* edited by Micah L. Issit, H.W. Wilson, 2019, pp.111-115.

APA: Brewer, E. (2019). Can the U.S. reinstate "maximum pressure" on North Korea? In Micah L. Issit (Ed.), *The reference shelf: The two Koreas* (pp. 111-115). Ipswich, MA: H.W. Wilson.

Embrace the Moon Miracle: Why Trump Should Let the Koreas Build Peace

By Daniel R. DePetris

The National Interest, December 4, 2018

There is no beating around the bush: nuclear talks between the United States and North Korea are not going particularly well. Stephen Biegun, the Trump administration's special envoy to North Korea, has yet to meet with his North Korean counterpart. All of the happy talk about Donald Trump striking a kinship with Kim Jong-un has been laughable at times; if the budding romance between the two was meant to butter Kim up to the point where he hands over his nuclear weapons, the strategy has clearly failed.

Inter-Korean negotiations, however, are another story. South Korean President Moon Jae-in has met with the North Korean dictator three times, with a fourth session that could be scheduled as soon as the end of the year. Such a high-level summit would have been unthinkable during the reign of his predecessor, who iced a sunshine policy South Korea's conservatives believed was foolish from the start. South and North Korean officials are talking like partners who want to improve the relationship rather than bickering like mortal enemies. The "Moon Miracle" is more than a motto—it has dramatically shifted North-South relations in less than a year.

North Korea hawks in Washington aren't especially thrilled about Moon's desire for reconciliation on the Korean Peninsula. One can assume National Security Adviser John Bolton, who penned an op-ed flirting with a preventative military strike on North Korea weeks before he was appointed, is not happy about it either. Yet the South Korean government is proceeding with the dialogue regardless, even if they are aware that going too far, too fast would earn a stern rebuke from the White House and very likely violate U.N. Security Council sanctions.

Washington and Seoul both agree that the Kim regime must denuclearize. But the countries have sincere disagreements about the best way to bring denuclearization about. Trump, like his predecessors, wants Pyongyang to give up the nukes before any sanctions are lifted. Moon's government believes peace and economic development in the North are prerequisites for denuclearization.

Moon Jae-in is right and Donald Trump—or at least Trump's national security aides—is wrong.

How do we know Trump has the wrong approach? Because outside of a missile and nuclear test moratorium (one that could quickly be reversed by Kim's order),

---

a few American prisoners being released, and a summit in Singapore that generated extensive airtime and a shiny press statement, nothing of substance on Kim's nuclear weapons has occurred. Pyongyang's nuclear program is still humming along, and none of us should have anticipated anything different. Kim has yet to sign a full agreement to change that; news that bomb fuel and missiles continue to be produced in facilities scattered throughout North Korea is, in fact, old news.

The White House continues to demand a full and honest declaration from Pyongyang of its nuclear assets before any sanctions relief or diplomatic concessions are granted. Yet as Siegfried Hecker has observed, to provide a to the Americans would be for Kim Jong-un to expose himself to a high risk for no gain. "A complete account of North Korea's nuclear weapons, materials, and facilities would, in Kim's view, likely be far too risky," Hecker wrote. "[I]t would essentially provide a targeting list for U.S. military planners and seal the inevitable end of the nuclear program and possibly his regime."

Trump is stuck. If he isn't willing to change his strategy, negotiations will remain bogged down until he loses his patience and walks away.

There is no trust at all between America and North Korea. However, there is at least some goodwill between the Koreans themselves. Both Koreas have embraced the kinds of confidence-building measures that can build a rapport between them. These include decreasing tension along the demilitarized zone (DMZ) and transforming the Korean Peninsula into a more predictable place. Guard posts along the border have been blown up. Joint railroad surveys are being conducted. Meetings are being regularized. A no-fly zone has been declared over the DMZ. Furthermore, talks are commencing about drawing final borders in waters that have been contested by both. None of this may involve nuclear weapons, but none of it should be dismissed as window dressing either.

> **Both Koreas have embraced the kinds of confidence-building measures that can build a rapport between them.**

The time has come for Donald Trump to follow Moon Jae-in's lead. Assuming North Korea's denuclearization is even plausible, it most certainly won't occur by 2021. The process will be long, frustrating, and tediously technical—and it could very well last over a decade.

What the United States can do right now, however, is support Seoul's peace initiative with the North. This will require tough choices by Washington, such as allowing certain cross-border projects to proceed and permitting the South Koreans to engage in some modest economic activity without having sanctions wielded over their heads.

Many hawks won't like it, most of whom have advocated for the same unconditional hardline status-quo which has failed over the last quarter-century.

If Trump wants to be the unconventional dealmaker he always claims to be, it's time for him to focus on helping the two Koreas solidify peace now instead of obstructing it in favor of an immediate denuclearization that will never come. The president doesn't have much time to waste; Trump reportedly hopes to embark on his second summit meeting with Kim early next year, so any change in strategy will need to be out in place well before that session occurs. To continue the current strategy is to continue failure, returning the world to the bad old days of 2016 and 2017 when U.S. and North Korean officials were trading insults.

Print Citations

CMS: DePetris, Daniel R. "Embrace the Moon Miracle: Why Trump Should Let the Koreas Build Peace." In *The Reference Shelf: The Two Koreas,* edited by Micah L. Issit, 116-118. Ipswich, MA: H.W. Wilson, 2019.

MLA: DePetris, Daniel R. "Embrace the Moon Miracle: Why Trump Should Let the Koreas Build Peace." *The Reference Shelf: The Two Koreas,* edited by Micah L. Issit, H.W. Wilson, 2019, pp. 116-118.

APA: DePetris, D.R. (2019). Embrace the Moon miracle: Why Trump should let the Koreas build peace. In Micah L. Issit (Ed.), *The reference shelf: The two Koreas* (pp. 116-118). Ipswich, MA: H.W. Wilson.

5
Korean Americans

All photos via Wikimedia.

Clockwise from top left: Judy Joo, host of *Food Network*'s "Korean Food Made Simple" (Mauritzio Mortiani); David Chang, restaurateur and television personality (David Shankbone); Steven Choi (R), former mayor and California assemblyman (City of Irvine); Paull Shin (D), first Korean American elected to Washington state legislature, (U.S. Navy); Map of Korean settlement in the U.S., 2000 (U.S. Census Bureau); Korean Americans in Koreatown, New York City (Chensiyuan).

Korea in America

There is no way to accurately encapsulate Korean Americans or the Korean American experience, because there is no archetypical Korean American. With nearly 2 million individuals of Korean descent living in the United States, the Korean American population is diverse and growing and has, since World War II, become an increasingly prominent minority in American society. Some Korean Americans, like John Cho and Jamie Chung, have reached the upper echelons of America's entertainment industry, while others have become major figures in business, technology, or science. Some Korean Americans trace their ancestry back to the North, some to the South, some to rural farming communities, others to the Korean Peninsula's bustling metropolises. The diversity of the Korean American reflects the diversity of experiences and cultures found within the Korean Peninsula.

The Macro Perspective

According to Pew Research, there were roughly 1.8 million Koreans living in the United States in 2015. More than 74 percent of those living in the United States had resided in the nation for at least 10 years, with the population of new arrivals gradually falling since the early 2000s. In general, roughly 63 percent of the population are fluent in English, including 94 percent of those who were born in the United States, compared to roughly 47 percent of those who were born in the Korean peninsula. In general, the Korean American population has similar educational attainment and lower poverty rates than the average for all Americans, and Korean Americans tend to have higher than average earnings. While most Korean Americans have settled in cities on the West Coast, there are significant populations of Korean Americans in many American cities, from the more than 200,000 in New York City to 61,000 living in Chicago, Illinois.[1]

To understand the history of Korean immigration, it is necessary to understand the prevalent patterns that have shaped American immigration policy and migration within the Korean Peninsula. From the mid-1800s to the 1960s, American immigration policy was based, to a large degree, on racial prejudice. Chinese immigrants were banned, entirely, in the 1800s. Federal policies regarding race and Asian immigration began with the 1882 Chinese Exclusion Act, which was passed as a temporary measure, but was later made permanent, and completely prohibited any Chinese individuals from immigrating into the United States. Following this act, Asian immigrants continued coming from other regions, including significant numbers of Japanese and Korean immigrants arriving in California. Business leaders embraced this influx, as they were able to pay limited wages for immigrant workers to replace the banned Chinese laborers who had been essential in Westward Expansion. Following the Russo-Japanese War of 1904-05, there was a short-term influx of Korean immigrants who fled the Japanese occupation of the Korean peninsula. Most of these immigrants, like the Japanese immigrants, found work in West Coast agricultural or railroad industries. Some Korean immigrants staged a Korean independence movement in exile and campaigned for the end to the Japanese occupation of their home country. Racial prejudice against Japanese and Korean Americans began to intensify, especially along the West Coast, leading to a ban on Japanese immigration in 1907.

Racial immigration policies were, and remain, a product of the American conservative movement. There have always been, and still are, those who believe that the preservation of American culture requires a balance of races in which white Americans of European descent remain the nation's largest and most politically powerful ethnic group. Whether or not racial balance is beneficial to America is subjective, but has been a dominant force in the history of American immigration policy. In the 1920s, this belief became law, which essentially banned all Asian immigration, severely limited other nonwhite immigration, but permitted immigration of white Europeans.[2]

America's racially-based quotas for immigration and the ban on Asian immigrants meant that, even while Americans and South Koreans fought together to defend South Korea from a communist takeover between 1950 and 1953, America's allies in South Korea were still predominantly prohibited from coming to the United States. Following the Korean War, both South and North Korea became military dictatorships and adopted severe policies with regard to the movement of citizens. While the South Korean military alliance with the United States made it more likely that South Koreans would be able to legally migrate, North Korea and the United States essentially remained enemy states from 1950 to the modern day and thus immigration of North Korean citizens to the United States was strictly banned.

The Immigration Act of 1965, established during a wave of political progressivism in the United States, removed the ban on Asian immigration and, for the first time in America's history, opened the door to Korean immigrants. Between 1970 and 1980, the population of Korean immigrants increased seven-fold from around 39,000 to over 290,000. The population then doubled again, over the next decade, reaching nearly 568,000 by 1990. Numbers peaked in 2010, at approximately 1.1 million. In 2015, the last year for which data is available, the population of Korean immigrants was estimated at approximately 1 million. As of 2018, Korean immigrants constitute some 2.4 percent of the 43.3 million immigrants living in the United States. Over the decades, as South Korea became more affluent, the socioeconomic status of Korean immigrants changed, and in the twenty-first century, Korean Americans are among the most successful of America's immigrant groups, achieving higher than average education levels and socioeconomic standing. The reduction in Korean immigration between 2010 and 2015 is largely the result of improving conditions in South Korea, which limits the appeal of migrating to the United States. While immigration is desireable for many Koreans, the fact that immigrants in the United States still face significant racial prejudice and other barriers from cultural integration reduces the allure of immigration.[3]

Getting In and Fitting In

In the November 2018 U.S. mid-term elections, six Korean American candidates, a record number, pursued federal office. The candidates included four Democrats, Andy Kim of New Jersey, David J. Kim of Georgia, Donna Mercado Kim, of Hawaii, and Dan Koh of Massachusetts, and two Republicans, Young Kim of California, and Pearl Kim of Pennsylvania. Though only Andy Kim was successful in his electoral bid, becoming only the second Korean American to win a seat in the US Congress, the fact that six candidates ran for office reflects the growing visibility of Korean Americans in US culture and the increasing diversity of America's public and political spheres of influence.[4]

The first Korean American elected to office was Republican Jay Kim, a South Korean-born engineer who was a surprise victor in the 1992 California legislative elections, and left a highly controversial legacy. In 1998, Kim, only the third federal legislator to be convicted of federal crimes while in office, was accused of accepting more than $250,000 in illegal foreign and corporate contributions. It was later revealed that Kim was connected to the highest number of campaign finance violations of any congressional candidate and that more than one-third of the contributions to his 1992 campaign came from illegal corporate sources, in return for Kim's support of corporate interests while in office.[5]

While it is likely that Kim never would have been elected without his illegal campaign activities, New Jersey's Andy Kim presents a sharp-contrast to his predecessor. Andy Kim entered the Democratic Party and embraced progressive approaches to public policy. Kim became a Rhodes Scholar, with a doctorate in international relations from the University of Oxford and worked in Afghanistan as an advisor to Generals David Petraeus and John Allen, before taking a position under the Obama administration for the National Security Council. More experienced and accomplished than the other 2018 candidates for office, Andy Kim won the election and marked a new era for Korean Americans in the US government.[6]

Even though Andy Kim was the only successful Korean American candidate in 2018, the spectrum of candidates is another reflection of the diversity of Korean American culture. With four running as Democrats and two as Republicans, Korean Americans have embraced both American progressivism and conservatism. For some, conservatism is a draw because of a shared belief in social conservative ideals, such as the primacy of family or adherence to religious beliefs. Speaking to the *Los Angeles Times*, Korean American residents Paul and Julianne Choi, both supporters of failed GOP candidate Young Kim, said of their choice, "Her agenda is very conservative, very family-oriented and Christian-minded values that Americans have cherished for a long time."[7] The Choi's also expressed support for Donald Trump, his position on immigration and religious freedom, and hoped that, if elected, Young Kim would support Trump's agenda.

On the other hand, many Korean Americans have distanced themselves from the conservative movement's attitudes about racial and ethnic diversity. Korean Americans, like all Asian Americans, face racial prejudice living in the United States and American conservative politicians and pundits are the primary vector for prejudicial attitudes about race in politics. For instance, Korean and Lebanese-American candidate Dan Koh of Massachusetts said of his candidacy, "My family has always very much valued public service and really believed that government can and should be a force for good for people." Towards this end, Koh supported enacting a higher minimum wage, investing in small businesses and entrepreneurship, and fighting for universal healthcare coverage, maintaining abortion rights, and supporting the Affordable Care Act, core expressions of American progressive values.[8]

This diversity in ideology is reflected in the way that Korean Americans have reacted to the Trump administration's attitudes towards North Korea. While some support Trump's rhetoric, sharing the belief that the North Korean regime should be prohibited from developing weapons of mass destruction, others are skeptical of Trump's policies and have little faith that the GOP would support the Korean people in the event of war or regime change. Many Korean Americans have family in Korea, and the Trump administration's attitudes about immigration in general, and nonwhite immigrants in particular is concerning. While potential reunification of North and South Korea continues to be an issue for both Korean Americans, and Koreans living in both states, the road to unification remains a divisive issue for both Korean Americans and for the the American population as a whole.

Overall, studies indicate that Korean Americans, once strongly aligned with conservatism, are increasingly shifting their allegiance towards the Democratic Party and progressive political positions in general. Overwhelmingly, younger Korean Americans identify as liberal and 2016 studies indicate that at least 54 percent of Korean Americans as a whole identify as Democrats. This demographic shift follows patterns among other nonwhite groups of Americans over the past 50 years as the Republican Party and American conservatism, in general, has become more closely aligned with racial and cultural isolationism, pushing nonwhite individuals, such as Hispanic and Asian Americans, out of the GOP and away from American conservatism in general.[9]

The political alignment of the Korean American population is but one reflection of the diversity within the Korean American population. While some work in blue collar positions, or as agricultural or industrial laborers, others are increasingly involved in America's cutting edge industries. Tim Hwang, founder of the Washington D.C.-based startup FiscalNote, which provides legal analytics, was born to Korean immigrants who settled in Bethesda, Maryland. He told *NBC News* that he and other Asian Americans entrepreneurs still face challenges of discrimination, in comparison to white-entrepreneurs in similar fields. Hwang described how the outsider status of immigrant entrepreneurs can erode one's self confidence and has a subtle limiting effect on one's potential for success. For instance, Hwang said that while AsianAmerican entrepreneurs like himself might be just as successful as other entrepreneurs inside the "boardroom," that there is a second level to advancement in society, the deals that take place between work "friends" over drinks or while golfing, from which outsiders like himself are typically excluded because of their differences from the familiar culture of American executives.[10]

While 2018 marked a tenuous time for Korean Americans given the tense political dialogue between Trump and North Korean leader Kim Jong-Un, the year was certainly a landmark in terms of Asian American representation and visibility. The surprise hit romantic comedy *Crazy Rich Asians* was one of the best-reviewed films of the year, a major blockbuster in theatres, and a breakout for a host of rising Asian American stars, including New York native Nora Lum, aka Awkwafina, daughter of a Chinese American father and South Korean mother, the latest Korean American to reach the upper echelons of American celebrity.[11] The success of *Crazy Rich Asians* follows in the wake of the television series *Fresh off the Boat*, which debuted in 2015 and is the first hit TV show starring, created by, and focusing on the lives of Asian Americans. Main star, actor Randall Park, a Los Angeles native born to Korean parents, became one of the most visible Korean American celebrities of the 2010s.

Visibility and representation are important components of identity, and thus the degree to which Korean Americans, and Asian Americans in general, feel represented in American media, education, business, and politics, is an important contributor in determining the degree to which Asian Americans feel *American* and that they are able to play a role in the nation's present and future. Over more than a century, Korean immigrants have been coming to the United States, enduring challenges and often facing prejudice in order to find opportunities for themselves or their families. Over the course of this long history, Korean Americans have farmed America's fields, pioneered new medicine and technology, served in the nation's government and military, and have, in general, lived American lives, some extraordinary, some ordinary, but all unique and all uniquely American.

Works Used

"2018 Candidates for Congress." *KAA*. Korean Americans in Action. 2018. Retrieved from https://kaaction.org/2018-candidates-for-congress/.

"Asian Americans Then and Now." *Asia Society*. Center for Global Education. 2018. Retrieved from https://asiasociety.org/education/asian-americans-then-and-now.

"Awkwafina of *Crazy Rich Asians* on Her Breakout Year: 'There Was This Idea That We Were Doing Something Big.'" *SCMP*. South China Morning Post. Dec 17, 2018. Retrieved from https://www.scmp.com/culture/film-tv/article/2178285/awkwafina-crazy-rich-asians-her-breakout-year-there-was-idea-we-were.

Eilperin, Juliet. "Days in the Life of Jay Kim in the U.S. House of Correction." *The Washington Post*. The Washington Post Co. May 22, 1998. Retrieved from https://www.washingtonpost.com/wp-srv/politics/campaigns/keyraces98/stories/ca052298.htm.

Fuchs, Chris. "Dan Koh's Family Taught Him Government 'Should Be a Force for Good.'" *NBC News*. NBC. May 16, 2018. Retrieved from https://www.nbcnews.com/news/asian-america/dan-koh-s-family-taught-him-government-should-be-force-n861476?icid=related.

Fuchs, Chris. "There Hasn't Been a Korean American in Congress Since 1999: Come November, There Could Be 4." *NBC News*. NBC. Aug 28, 2018. Retrieved from https://www.nbcnews.com/news/asian-america/there-hasn-t-been-korean-american-congress-1999-come-november-n904211.

"Koreans in the U.S. Fact Sheet." *Pew Social Trends*. Pew Research Center. Sep 8, 2017. Retrieved from http://www.pewsocialtrends.org/fact-sheet/asian-americans-koreans-in-the-u-s/.

Mai-Duc, Christine. "A Young Kim Supporter Values Her 'Very Conservative' Viewpoints." *Los Angeles Times*. Nov 6, 2018. Retrieved from https://www.latimes.com/politics/la-na-pol-midterm-election-day-updates-a-kim-supporter-values-her-very-1541539603-htmlstory.html.

Rode, Erin. "Increasing Numbers of Korean Americans Are Identifying as Democrats." *USC Annenberg Media*. University of Southern California. Apr 28, 2018. Retrieved from http://www.uscannenbergmedia.com/2018/04/28/increasing-numbers-of-korean-americans-are-identifying-as-democrats/.

Shang, Eva. "CEOs in the Making: The Youngest Asian-Americans in Tech." *NBC News*. NBC. Feb 22, 2016. Retrieved from https://www.nbcnews.com/news/asian-america/ceos-making-youngest-asian-americans-tech-n516691.

Zong, Jie and Jeanne Batalova. "Korean Immigrants in the United States." *MPI*. Migration Policy Institute. Feb 8, 2017. Retrieved from https://www.migrationpolicy.org/article/korean-immigrants-united-states.

Notes

1. "Koreans in the U.S. Fact Sheet," *Pew Research Center*.
2. "Asian Americans Then and Now," *Asia Society*.
3. Zong and Batalova, "Korean Immigrants in the United States."
4. "2018 Candidates for Congress," *KAA*.
5. Eilperin, "Days in the Life of Jay Kim in the U.S. House of Correction."
6. Fuchs, "There Hasn't Been a Korean American in Congress since 1999: Come November, There Could Be 4."
7. Mai-Duc, "A Young Kim Supporter Values Her 'Very Conservative' Viewpoints."
8. Fuchs, "Dan Koh's Family Taught Him Government 'Should Be a Force for Good.'"
9. Rode, "Increasing Numbers of Korean Americans Are Identifying as Democrats."
10. Shang, "CEO's in the Making: The Youngest Asian-Americans in Tech."
11. "Awkwafina of Crazy Rich Asians on Her Breakout Year: 'There Was This Idea That We Were Doing Something Big," *SCMP*.

Awe, Gratitude, Fear: Conflicting Emotions for Korean-Americans in the Era of Trump

By Jennifer Medina

The New York Times, May 20, 2018

BUENA PARK, Calif.—When it comes to immigration, Sylvia Kim has been a fierce opponent of President Trump. She has protested him at L.A.X. airport and written about his "shameful legacy" on refugees. But on Thursday Ms. Kim watched the dramatic events out of North Korea unfold with a mixture of shock and gratitude.

"To say it is extremely historic is an understatement," she said.

Southern California is home to the largest Korean population outside of Asia and Ms. Kim is one of many Korean-Americans here feeling a whipsaw of emotions over the administration's actions in recent days. While the president has infuriated some with his policies and rhetoric on immigration, others are hopeful that his approach to foreign affairs could help bring peace to a long-divided region where the vast majority of Korean-Americans still have relatives.

"It is very conflicting because what he is doing domestically is so horrendous on so many levels," said Ms. Kim, the Orange County director for Asian Americans Advancing Justice, a civil-rights group. "Yet on the international level he might achieve something nobody else has."

The Korean meeting, which Mr. Trump announced on Thursday, is the most promising sign in years for stability in the region, which has prompted an outpouring of support and celebration among many Korean-Americans. But many others—particularly younger Korean immigrants and the children of immigrants—are more focused on the fight against his domestic agenda. It has created deep divisions between those who admire the president and those who see his administration as a threat.

"It's a question of priorities: No matter how important immigration is, nuclear war was always the higher danger," added Ms. Kim, who also works with North Korean human rights groups.

There are roughly 325,000 Koreans in Southern California, with about one-third in Orange County, where they have thrived in suburban enclaves. In Buena Park, a bustling business district serves as a kind of suburban Koreatown, offering an endless array of restaurants along with K-pop dance studios and a Korean movie theater.

Their powerful economic influence obscures another fact: Roughly 20 percent of Korean immigrants are unauthorized. Immigrants from South Korea make up the fifth-largest share of DACA recipients, and the number of undocumented immigrants coming from the country has increased by more than 700 percent in the last 30 years. Now many young Koreans are embracing roles as immigration activists.

The fight over immigration, however, is of little interest to many older Korean immigrants who arrived in the United States decades ago. Instead, they have been captivated by the momentous developments in their native country, after three detainees were released by North Korea this week.

"This is more than stopping nuclear proliferation for us—it is very personal," said Ellen Ahn, the executive director of Korean Community Services, based in Buena Park. Ms. Ahn's mother, who was a refugee from North Korea in the 1950s, walked south for days to escape the country when she was 9 years old. Ms. Ahn said she grew up hearing stories of her grandfather being captured by the North Korean Army. "It's really recent history for our families, all of those kinds of memories are etched in our collective family consciousness."

Like many of her friends, she stayed up all night watching the Korean-language news on the meeting last month between the leaders of North and South Korea. She texted her 73-year-old mother at 2 a.m. to see if she was watching. "She told me she was in her 12th hour and had been crying the entire time."

The next morning, her parents went out to celebrate by eating Pyongyang-style cold noodles—the kind the North Korean leader, Kim Jong-un, brought to a banquet during the meeting with President Moon Jae-in.

"To see what is happening is joyous and dramatic," she added. Ms. Ahn said that fissures between the generations over the Trump administration are not just over issues like immigration; they are also about language. Younger Koreans raised in America rely on English-language media, while older generations voraciously consume news directly from South Korean sources. "People have divided energies," she said.

Korean-American citizens have historically not been a politically active voting block: Nationally, about 46 percent of eligible voters nationally cast a ballot in 2016, compared with 61 percent among adult citizens overall. This year, though, their vote could be crucial in several competitive congressional races in Orange County.

Statewide, roughly 54 percent of Koreans self-identify as Democrats, according to the National Asian-American Survey, far more reliably liberal than immigrants from China and Vietnam. Nationally, 75 percent of Koreans voted for Hillary Clinton in 2016, according to the same survey.

John Kim, who leads the Korean Federation of Orange County, said he voted for Mr. Trump in part because he believed his business background would help him solve intractable problems, like the Korean conflict.

"I supported him because he said he would do something," Mr. Kim said. "He is honest and he is doing what he said he would do. He does not stand for nonsense. So to see this now, it is a relief."

But among critics, anger toward Mr. Trump runs deep. Some view his past comments as racist, pointing to an incident earlier this year when he asked a Korean-American intelligence official, "Where are you from?" When she said she was from

New York, he pressed to know where "your people" are from, suggesting the "pretty Korean lady" should negotiate with North Korea.

After Mr. Trump's pre-dawn news conference on the tarmac, Korean-American leaders all over the country were struggling with how to rectify the White House's paradoxical positions.

"We see there are various, blatant contradictions in his general attitude and disposition," said John Park, 44, the executive director of the MinKwon Center for Community Action, the leading Korean-American activist group in New York.

"In terms of North and South Korea, we do care about family unification; that's something we've been hoping for, for a long time," Mr. Park said. But, he added, "They are O.K. with splitting up families. They are really doubling down on that position, which is horrifying and inhumane to us."

Even among those who support negotiations with North Korea, some Korean-Americans say they are skeptical the Trump administration will play a crucial role. Jung-woo Kim, who moved to Fullerton from South Korea when he was 15 and regularly speaks to friends there, said that it was Mr. Moon, the South Korean president, who deserved credit for the recent shifts.

> **Even among those who support negotiations with North Korea, some Korean-Americans say they are skeptical the Trump administration will play a crucial role.**

"If you want to have peace, it's Korean people's work to do," said Mr. Kim, who now works for the National Korean American Service & Education Consortium. "Whatever he is doing is not about helping our people. He thinks he deserves the Nobel Prize."

Mr. Kim is among the activists who hope the fight over immigration will play a key role in the midterm congressional races in Orange County, where Democrats are trying win several seats. Local political experts say Korean voters in the county are evenly split, with about a third each registering as Republican[s] and Democrats and the remainder choosing neither party.

Earlier this year, dozens of people gathered outside Representative Mimi Walters's district office, urging her to do more to create a path to citizenship. Since Mr. Trump's election, the activists have focused their ire on Ms. Walters, along with other Republicans in Orange County who are facing tough re-election bids this year.

"They haven't done very much for us, even though there are so many people here impacted," said Erica Kim, who has lived in Orange County for years and now works as a parent organizer at the Korean Resource Center. "My daughter thinks she is American. My friends, they want to do something to help her. I tell them: The only way we can change anything is vote and get people who are elected to listen."

Print Citations

CMS: Medina, Jennifer. "Awe, Gratitude, Fear: Conflicting Emotions for Korean-Americans in the Era of Trump." In *The Reference Shelf: The Two Koreas*, edited by Micah L. Issit, 127-130. Ipswich, MA: H.W. Wilson, 2019.

MLA: Medina, Jennifer. "Awe, Gratitude, Fear: Conflicting Emotions for Korean-Americans in the Era of Trump." *The Reference Shelf: The Two Koreas,* edited by Micah L. Issit, H.W. Wilson, 2019, pp. 127-130.

APA: Medina, J. (2019). Awe, gratitude, fear: Conflicting emotions for Korean-Americans in the era of Trump. In Micah L. Issit (Ed.), *The reference shelf: The two Koreas* (pp. 127-130). Ipswich, MA: H.W. Wilson.

North Korea Defectors, Resettled in the US, Torn as Tensions Escalate

By Shachar Peled
CNN, September 17, 2017

(CNN)—As North Korea continues to boast of its military power with missile launches and bomb tests, resettled defectors from the totalitarian nation are torn: Some hope for an end to the vocal hostilities between North Korea and the United States, while others wish the tense rhetoric would result in military action against the regime of Kim Jong Un.

"If I think about it politically, for future freedom, then I'm hoping North Korea will shoot a missile to somewhere and then the US or the South Korean government will take action," Grace Jo, a North Korean defector living in Maryland, told *CNN*.

Jo, 26, grew up in North Korea in the 1990s at the height of the famine years, which killed around 1 million people, according to experts on the isolated country. She lost her father and four siblings before fleeing with her mother and older sister to China, and from there sought asylum in the United States.

Like many other human rights activists raising awareness of conditions for North Koreans, Jo has grown frustrated.

"The North Korean regime should not exist," she said fervently. "For many years, nothing has been accomplished politically. We have to find a way to shut down the leader and the military power."

Jo said she doesn't want to see innocent people killed, and she expressed concern for the citizens of North Korea, but for the long run, she said, military action is necessary. The harsh language coming from the Trump administration gives her hope.

"The strong words maybe will work. Before, all the presidents tried to treat North Korea in a nicer way and it won't work," she said.

Young Sik Kim, 73, who now lives in Virginia, agreed the United States should go to war with his homeland. He fled in 1985, going first to China, then Russia, before arriving to the United States in 2011.

"I think Kim Jong Un is a young child," he told *CNN* via an interpreter in a conference call. "He doesn't know what he's doing."

Growing up an orphan under the regime of Kim Il Sung—grandfather of the current leader, and founder of the dynasty that has ruled North Korea since 1948—Young Sik Kim remembers a different country. He said the older leader took care of his people by investing in agriculture, while his grandson is focused solely on investing in nuclear weapons.

He acknowledged the high cost of war to the land and people, but said he is determined that North Korea should be "wiped out and reconstructed."

A Divided Community

Joseph Kim, 27, who is still searching for the sister and mother he lost when they fled to China, holds a different approach.

"I feel really sad for this political language. The words that have been exchanged between Pyongyang and Washington are ridiculous," he told *CNN* from Washington, where he is on an internship between semesters of political studies at Bard College.

"I hope both leaders realize it's a matter of thousands and thousands of lives and it would be tragic if anything happens with a military conflict," he said.

Joseph Kim defected from North Korea to the United States in 2007.

Kim's father died of starvation, prompting his sister and mother to cross the border to China in search of food and work. He hasn't seen them since.

Kim fled to China three years later and made his way to the United States with the help of an activist. He delivered a TED talk in 2013 detailing the story of his life in North Korea during the famine years, and the online version has surpassed 2 million views.

"I still haven't given up hope to see you," he said as he teared up during his TED talk, directing his words at his sister.

Kim shares Jo's frustrations but said he thinks the possibility of a nuclear war is unbearable. He wishes for a more restrained approach when it comes to President Trump.

"I hope he realizes that what he says matters and has significant meaning to the general American public and the rest of world," he said. "I don't think such provocative statements produce any good results."

Defector: Trump Must "Stop Kim Jong Un"

Charles Kim, 48, spent six months in a North Korean prison. He had fled to China, was caught and sent back across the border, but persisted in his attempts.

"Once you get a taste of what freedom is like, it's like drugs—you're going to do it again," he said through his interpreter. "In prison you are not treated like a human. You are not really alive. You work all day and hardly have any food."

Charles Kim said he was forced to bury executed inmates while in prison. He cut all ties with his family because "even if you're released, your family will have a bad name and your children will face government oppression."

Despite leaving behind his son and ex-wife, Charles Kim—today a resident of Charlottesville, Virginia—is a proponent of an American action. He thinks the North Korean dictator is taking advantage of the American democratic system.

"Kim Jong Un knows that even if Trump says he's going to war he cannot, because in a democracy there are different groups and if enough people won't agree, Trump won't be able to do it," he said.

> **Some hope for an end to the vocal hostilities between North Korea and the United States, while others wish the tense rhetoric would result in military action against the regime of Kim Jong Un.**

As far as he is concerned, Charles Kim said, Trump could not be tougher in words or actions when it comes to human rights violations in his country. "At this developed stage, Trump needs to do everything he can to stop Kim Jong Un," he said.

Long Road to Freedom

According to Lindsay Lloyd, deputy director of the Human Freedom Initiative at the Bush Institute, there are around 225 "direct" North Korean refugees who have received asylum in the United States following the North Korean Human Rights Act of 2004. These defectors usually go through China and then to Southeast Asia, where they apply for asylum.

Another 250 North Koreans in the United States arrived as legal immigrants after spending several months or years in South Korea, and obtaining a South Korean citizenship. Despite being born in North Korea, they are registered as South Koreans on America's doorstep, Lloyd said.

As for undocumented immigrants from North Korea, they are "all over the map," Lloyd said, estimating they are fewer than 1,000.

A 2014 Bush Institute research revealed North Koreans also have conflicting feelings regarding their assimilation and opportunities in the United States.

"In many cases, the support provided to refugees in the United States was stellar and participants believed the help they received, despite the challenges they faced, allowed them to very quickly achieve economic independence," the report stated.

"For others, however, outside help was scarce and it was not only a struggle to acclimate to their new surroundings, but to achieve a minimal standard of financial independence," the report said.

Print Citations

CMS: Peled, Shachar. "North Korean Defectors, Resettled in the US, Torn as Tensions Escalate." In *The Reference Shelf: The Two Koreas*, edited by Micah L. Issit, 131-134. Ipswich, MA: H.W. Wilson, 2019.

MLA: Peled, Shachar. "North Korean Defectors, Resettled in the US, Torn as Tensions Escalate." *The Reference Shelf: The Two Koreas,* edited by Micah L. Issit, H.W. Wilson, 2019, pp. 131-134.

APA: Peled, S. (2019). North Korean defectors, resettled in the US, torn as tensions escalate. In Micah L. Issit (Ed.), *The reference shelf: The two Koreas* (pp. 131-134). Ipswich, MA: H.W. Wilson.

North Korean Defectors See American Dream Deferred as Reality Sets in the US

By Soo Youn
The Guardian, June 13, 2016

When Chang Ho Kim was living in North Korea, information trickled in from China about the world outside the closed country. Through the lens of pirated movies, he says, America had looked to Kim like "a very rich and luxurious place."

In 1997, at the height of a famine that killed around one million people, Kim escaped with his wife into China, then Mongolia, then to South Korea.

Defectors from the North automatically become South Korean citizens after a mandatory three-month transition that is part debriefing, part re-education. Most North Korean defectors in the South stand out, and the Kims were no exception. They have distinct accents, and are often shorter and slighter with darker, sallow skin from years of malnutrition. It's hard to avoid South Koreans' prejudice and suspicions that North Koreans are spies.

Remembering the Hollywood images of the US, the Kims decided to make their way to the US illegally through a broker.

But for the Kims, and others like them, life in the US is not necessarily easier.

The American celluloid dream comes with skyrocketing price tags. North Koreans arrive with little or no experience of bills, rent, and no means to cope with the lack of social services and health insurance that illegal immigrants must navigate.

"American life is so hard. Money, money, money," said Pastor Young Gu Kim, an evangelical South Korean immigrant who helps defectors. "Some defectors told me, 'Oh pastor, sometimes I miss it over there.'"

Like Chang Ho Kim, many North Koreans enter illegally and settle in Los Angeles, amid the large population of ethnic Koreans. Nearly 200 former North Koreans live in Los Angeles, advocacy groups say, but exact numbers are unknown.

"South Korea has an enormous program to resettle North Koreans. It's basically a yearlong program, but then it goes on beyond that in many ways where there are grants for education, for housing, and all kinds of things," said Lindsay Lloyd, who currently leads the George W Bush Institute's Freedom in North Korea project. "So the scale of their programs to bring these people into South Korea, compared to what happens here in the US, it's just radically, radically different."

In South Korea, refugees received a few thousand dollars to start their new lives and learned skills most people take for granted: grocery shopping or using an ATM.

"When refugees come to the United States ... the US government only provides about six months' worth of support for them," Lloyd added. "It's done through groups like Catholic charities and others that really just address the basics: find a place to live, get some basic healthcare, maybe some rudimentary English lessons, a first job, that kind of thing."

The State Department has documented 192 North Koreans entering the US from 1 January 2002 to 1 January 2016. But this only includes refugees who have obtained green cards through the North Korean Human Rights Act of 2004.

As undocumented immigrants, Kim's family live in a two-bedroom apartment in LA's Koreatown. Previously, they shared the unit with another North Korean family who have since moved back to South Korea. Kim's wife works full-time at a massage parlor where he works part-time. Korean churches and community groups offer aid and small cash payments from time to time.

A couple years ago, the family was about to be deported, said Kim, who has changed his name since arriving in the US. But they were able to stay on a U visa for crime victims. The visa enabled them to receive "food stamps, the best thing about America," he said. He thinks the country should do more for North Koreans, providing money and benefits.

Lloyd said Kim's thinking was not surprising coming from someone who lived in a Communist state.

"It's understandable that somebody coming out of that background would have very different expectations about what the government is supposed to do for them."

North Koreans in the US experience feelings of isolation, experts say, that's exacerbated by a lack of community. A large tide of South Koreans emigrated to the US in the 1960s and 1970s, after the Korean war, and old prejudices and suspicions toward North Koreans linger.

> **North Koreans arrive with little or no experience of bills, rent, and no means to cope with the lack of social services and health insurance that illegal immigrants must navigate.**

In October 2014, the Bush Institute at the George W Bush Presidential Center published a qualitative survey, "US-Based North Korean Refugees." It found that "even those on a path to citizenship lived almost entirely within Korean communities," the survey reported. "However, nearly all also said they did not feel completely accepted or included, and often felt looked down upon or pitied."

"North Koreans, South Koreans—everyone thinks it's the same people," Pastor Kim said, but the two groups are "so different..

Ok Soon Joo is one of the fortunate ones with a green card. In September 2011, she arrived in the US. After escaping from North Korea on her second try, she spent several years in China, married to a Chinese man. She eventually escaped to a refugee camp in Thailand, where she was able to phone an aunt who had made it to America several months earlier.

"Luckily for me it only took 10 months" to reach America, she said. Because she had late-stage stomach cancer, her application was expedited. She arrived in Colorado and immediately had surgery. The cancer has been treated, but overall, she's not in great health.

When she left her small town in North Korea, she left her 12-year-old son and husband behind. Later she learned that they ran out of food and the boy went missing.

Joo spent years in China during which she had a six-year old daughter with the Chinese man. But she lived there undocumented and has no proof that she is the child's mother. She sends the girl a couple hundred dollars a month through her Chinese grandparents.

Life was hard in China, Joo said. "When you're in China, as a woman, your problems become worse. There's sexual trafficking and sexual slavery. There are people who are there to exploit the women that defect. Because you don't have a Chinese identification card on you, you have to do what the broker wants ... You lose any shred of human dignity."

Now 38, Joo works in a skincare shop and lives with her partner, a South Korean man, in Koreatown. She's grateful for her life in the US, but her thoughts are preoccupied with the past.

"Because we were born in North Korea, that title keeps haunting me," she said. "I'm wondering: did I commit many sins in a past life to be born in North Korea?"

Joo knows it's almost impossible to find her son, but she said she hopes she can reunite with her daughter. "I want to bring them here. I didn't come here to America just so I could live well by myself."

The North Koreans who have US citizenship may have the easiest time moving forward in their new lives.

Sammy Hyun, who was jailed in North Korea after trying to sneak back into the country, was able to escape with his family to a UN refugee camp in Beijing. Now a US citizen, he works as a sushi chef and lives in Koreatown with his six-year-old son Ari and his new wife.

Hyun, 40, said during an interview last year that he was happy in the US, where he's lived since 2007. The next day he was leaving to visit his older brother and sister in South Korea. He had bought them vitamins and dried fruit (a common gift for Korean Americans) from the big-box store Costco, which he described as "truly amazing."

When asked how he felt about his US passport, he answered in English: "Lucky."

Print Citations

CMS: Soo, Youn. "North Korean Defectors See American Dream Deferred as Reality Sets in the US." In *The Reference Shelf: The Two Koreas*, edited by Micah L. Issit, 135-138. Ipswich, MA: H.W. Wilson, 2019.

MLA: Soo, Youn. "North Korean Defectors See American Dream Deferred as Reality Sets in the US." *The Reference Shelf: The Two Koreas,* edited by Micah L. Issit, H.W. Wilson, 2019, pp. 135-138.

APA: Soo, Y. (2019). North Korean defectors see American dream deferred as reality sets in the US. In Micah L. Issit (Ed.), *The reference shelf: The two Koreas* (pp. 135-138). Ipswich, MA: H.W. Wilson.

Some Korean Americans Have a Personal Stake in Next Week's Summit: Finding Family

By Anna Fifield and Min Joo Kim
The Washington Post, June 7, 2018

SEOUL—For many Americans, President Trump's planned summit with North Korean leader Kim Jong Un this month isn't just political. It's personal.

That's because as many as 300,000 U.S. citizens of Korean descent can trace their family history to North Korea, or rather to the northern half of Korea.

And some are hoping that the summit will usher in a new period of warmer relations that will pave the way for family members to be reunited, or at least find out what happened to long-lost brothers and sisters.

"I am so old now and I suffered from pancreatic cancer last year, so the idea of meeting them feels very difficult to me," said Hyun-ock Seo, who is 87 and lives in a retirement home in Chicago. She hasn't seen her three younger siblings since the Korean War broke out in 1950.

"But just being able to know before I die whether they are still alive, that would be a big deal for me," she said.

She isn't too optimistic, especially since she heard a few years ago that her youngest brother had died of cancer. But she hasn't entirely given up hope.

Many families were separated during the Korean War, and that separation was cemented when the peninsula was definitively divided at the end of the conflict in 1953.

During periods of rapprochement between the two Koreas, the North has sometimes agreed to allow brief family reunions in which South Koreans cross the border for a few hours. The scenes from the reunions—brief encounters with a mother or brother not seen for six decades—are always heart-wrenching, exposing the human toll of what was supposed to be a temporary division.

But Korean Americans have been excluded from the more than two dozen inter-Korean reunions that have taken place since 1985.

Before the Trump administration imposed a travel ban last year, North Korea had permitted about 200 Americans to travel to the country to be reunited with family members—often only briefly, sometimes not at all—through a pro-North group called the Korean American National Coordinating Council.

Others have fallen prey to scammers offering to arrange meetings on China's border with North Korea.

Now, a group of young Korean Americans called Divided Families USA is urging the Trump administration to ask North Korea to allow reunions

> **Many families were separated during the Korean War, and that separation was cemented when the peninsula was definitively divided at the end of the conflict in 1953.**

between members of their grandparents' generation—Americans like Seo and their North Korean relatives.

"Our Korean American divided families are the only remaining human link between the United States and North Korea," said Paul Lee of Divided Families USA. "But time is running out for these elderly people, many of whom are nearing the end of their lives."

The group has compiled a list of 53 Americans, including Seo, who are willing to take part in a reunion pilot program, and the last known details of their family members in North Korea.

Seo last saw her two younger sisters and youngest brother at the end of 1950. She remembers a day of chaos and panic in their home town of Tanchon, on North Korea's east coast. People were flocking to the police station. Documents were being burned. She thought she was going to die.

Seo, who was 20, and two other brothers, who were 14 and 16, wanted to evacuate. But their mother would not go, concerned about her youngest three children still at home. The older siblings prevailed, and the four, including the mother, begged their way onto a South Korean army truck heading for the North Korean port of Hungnam, down the coast.

They became part of the Hungnam evacuation, boarding a southbound U.N. ship in an escape to the South that became known as "the Miracle of Christmas." South Korean President Moon Jae-in's parents were also on that ship.

They never saw the younger children again. But over the years, Seo—who left for the United States in 1983—was able to get letters and money to her sisters through brokers on the Chinese border.

She heard that Sun Ok, who would be 78 now, had become a writer and had a son who was good at sports. Chong Ja, who would be 76, was living in Pyongyang. But Mu Ung went to the Soviet Union, working as a logger, and reportedly died of cancer there.

The letters Seo received in return were filled with lavish praise for the Kim regime and tales of how wonderful life in North Korea was. She realized the letters were being read by censors and stopped sending her $500 remittances.

Still, Seo, who worked for years in a laundromat, and her husband, also an escapee from North Korea and separated from his brothers, never gave up hope of a reunion. They held on to their three-story house in Chicago long after their children had left home, keeping space for their siblings. Just in case.

After her husband died a few years ago without seeing his brothers, Seo gave the house to her son. Her hopes of hearing anything from her siblings now are rapidly fading.

Shawn Kim, who lives in the San Francisco area and works at Stanford University, is hoping to help her grandmother, who is 93, return to her home town, Haeju, just over the border in what is now North Korea.

"I tell her that the talks are going great, that Chairman Kim Jong Un is going to meet with Trump," said Kim, who took part in a peace march near the border last month. "She says she's very weak, but she would like to go back to her home town before she dies."

Kim's grandfather used to go to an observatory overlooking the border and just look across. Like Seo's husband, he never got to go back.

"It makes me really sad. I don't know how much time my grandma has left, and one of her wishes is to be able to know if her family is alive, to be able to see her home town one last time," Kim said. "So I'm pouring everything into that. Even if I have to wheel her across in a wheelchair."

Print Citations

CMS: Fifield, Anna, and Min Joo Kim. "Some Korean Americans Have a Personal Stake in Next Week's Summit: Finding Family." In *The Reference Shelf: The Two Koreas*, edited by Micah L. Issit, 139-141. Ipswich, MA: H.W. Wilson, 2019.

MLA: Fifield, Anna, and Min Joo Kim. "Some Korean Americans Have a Personal Stake in Next Week's Summit: Finding Family." *The Reference Shelf: The Two Koreas,* edited by Micah L. Issit, H.W. Wilson, 2019, pp. 139-141.

APA: Fifield, A., & Kim, M.J. (2019). South Korean Americans have a personal state in next week's summit: Finding family. In Micah L. Issit (Ed.), *The reference shelf: The two Koreas* (pp. 139-141). Ipswich, MA: H.W. Wilson.

Conan O'Brien Accidentally Exposed Culture Gap between Koreans and Korean-Americans

Quartz, April 13, 2016

Conan O'Brien's very special Korea episode, which aired on *TBS* over the weekend, is a much bigger deal than you might imagine (clips are available on TBS.com). It is as good a glimpse as you're likely to find of both the limitlessness and the limits of globalization in the year 2016. Conan is joined in this adventure by Korean-American actor Steven Yeun, who plays *The Walking Dead*'s scrappy Glenn Rhee. Yeun serves as the Virgil to Coco's Dante. They're two deadpan comedians in a country where people don't smile at anyone they don't know.

Now, Conan O'Brien basically wins the Nobel Prize in awkwardness, and he knows it. He would appear out of place even at a convention of ginger Irish-American comedians who went to Harvard in the 1980s—let alone the streets of Seoul. What most Americans wouldn't pick up on, however, is that Steven Yeun looks almost as out of place in Korea as Conan does.

Conan in Korea is also a snapshot of how three distinct cultural groups now view each other: Americans, Koreans, and Korean-Americans. And make no mistake, the latter two groups are increasingly non-overlapping.

You Are Not the Sasha Baron-Cohen in This Equation

Even though the late-night show *Conan* is not broadcast in Korea, its internet episodes have gained a cult following among the millennial Korean set; in fact, upon arriving at Incheon, airport he was greeted by 2,000 fans.

It's not hard to see why. Conan is a bit of a curiosity: A satirist who hates cynicism. "For the record, [cynicism] is my least favorite quality," he famously said on his final NBC *Tonight Show* episode in 2010. His treatment of Korea is respectful and at times educational (Coco is a known history buff). And it's a good thing, too, because when you are a Western comic visiting Korea, you are not the Sacha Baron-Cohen in this equation: Koreans are.

Comedian Jack Black learned this the hard way, when he was in Korea earlier this year promoting *Kung Fu Panda 3* and was subjected to all manner of humiliation on the Korean variety show *Infinite Challenge*. Chloë Grace Moretz, who guest-starred on Korea's iteration of *Saturday Night Live* earlier this year, was forced to

wear a traditional Korean out-
fit (while everyone else was
in regular Western dress), go
completely mental, and bitch-
slap a man with a wad of kimchi. (Google "kimchi slap."
It's a real thing.)

> **You might think that a Korean-American
> star visiting Korea might get a hero's
> welcome. But this is rarely the case.**

Conan, in turn, sang for his supper by starring in a K-pop music video alongside Steven Yeun (who can actually sing) and big-deal Korean recording artist JYP.
Conan also did a cameo on a popular K-drama *One More Happy Ending* (about aging girl K-pop stars), in which he plays a talking goldfish and unwelcome client at an
upscale Seoul matchmaking firm.

What's significant about this appearance is that Conan's character, a Westerner,
is even allowed to be a client at a Korean matchmaking firm. Miscegenation has
historically been taboo in Korea, only becoming barely permissible in recent years
due a rural female shortage and the inevitability of immigration.

In the context of the K-drama, the heroine is offput by Conan's familiarity, exag-
gerated bravado, and awkwardness. The white guy is never the hero.

Neither Fish nor Fowl

You might think that a Korean-American star visiting Korea might get a hero's welcome. But this is rarely the case.

Steven Yeun might well be the one of the most globally recognizable actors of
Korean descent. But within Korea, he doesn't conform to the ideal of a Korean
celebrity—for no real reason other than that he is unaffected, he hasn't had epican-
thic fold surgery on his eyelids, and his haircut cost less than $400. Going through
the Korean media coverage of Yeun, it's clear to me that Koreans don't know what
to do with him, even though his Korean is quite good. To Koreans, he is in that
awkward Korean-American category—neither fish nor fowl, inherently somewhat
untrustworthy. I have the same problem when I visit Korea; it's why I don't go there
unless I have to.

Besides which, trends change so rapidly in Korea that ex-pats can barely keep
up—not even with food trends. In one scene from the Conan special, Yeun is comi-
cally unable to identify any of the side dishes at a Seoul restaurant, leading Conan
to comment, "You're sort of like Anthony Bourdain if he knew absolutely nothing."

Zombie Fighting Is the True Meritocracy

For me, and I suspect for a lot of Asian Americans, the Conan in Korea episode was
as much about Steven Yeun as it was about Conan. Asian-Americans and particularly Korean-Americans see Steven Yeun as their embodiment of It Gets Better, in
perhaps the same way that African-Americans viewed Sidney Poitier in the 1960s. I
would go so far as to say that in entertainment and pop cultural terms, it's now the
1960s for Asian-Americans.

Oh, you think I'm exaggerating? How could America be 60 years behind in their acceptance of Korean (or Asian-) Americans? Well, here's one example: In 2006, when my novel *Kept: A Comedy of Sex and Manners* (Simon & Schuster) was published, my US agent met with a Hollywood agent to try to sell the movie rights. The Hollywood agent's response: "I don't see a movie being made with an Asian-American heroine." This was just 10 years ago, people.

So why, only four years later in 2010, was Steven Yeun able to get cast as a central character in what would become America's top-rated TV show for the last four years? Answer: historically, zombie-fighter has always been an equal-opportunity job. As I've written elsewhere, George Romero set the precedent for this, making the landmark decision of casting an African-American actor (Duane Jones) as the star and hero of his 1968 seminal zombie classic *Night of the Living Dead*. That movie just so happens to have come out the same year that the Civil Rights Act passed. This particular horror sub-genre, in other words, is the minority kingmaker.

Print Citations

CMS: "Conan O'Brien Accidentally Exposed Culture Gap between Koreans and Korean-Americans." In *The Reference Shelf: The Two Koreas*, edited by Micah L. Issit, 142-144. Ipswich, MA: H.W. Wilson, 2019.

MLA: "Conan O'Brien Accidentally Exposed Culture Gap between Koreans and Korean-Americans." *The Reference Shelf: The Two Koreas,* edited by Micah L. Issit, H.W. Wilson, 2019, pp. 142-144.

APA: Quartz. (2019). Conan O'Brien accidentally exposed culture gap between Koreans and Korean-Americans. In Micah L. Issit (Ed.), *The reference shelf: The two Koreas* (pp. 142-144). Ipswich, MA: H.W. Wilson.

Bibliography

"2018 Candidates for Congress." *KAA*. Korean Americans in Action. 2018. Retrieved from https://kaaction.org/2018-candidates-for-congress/.

Albert, Eleanor. "What to Know About the Sanctions on North Korea." *CFR*. Council on Foreign Relations. Jan 3, 2018. Retrieved from https://www.cfr.org/backgrounder/what-know-about-sanctions-north-korea.

Armstrong, Charles K. "Korean History and Political Geography." *Asia Society*. Center for Global Education. 2018. Retrieved from https://asiasociety.org/education/korean-history-and-political-geography.

"Asian Americans Then and Now." *Asia Society*. Center for Global Education. 2018. Retrieved from https://asiasociety.org/education/asian-americans-then-and-now.

"Awkwafina of *Crazy Rich Asians* on Her Breakout Year: 'There Was This Idea That We Were Doing Something Big.'" *SCMP*. South China Morning Post. Dec 17, 2018. Retrieved from https://www.scmp.com/culture/film-tv/article/2178285/awkwafina-crazy-rich-asians-her-breakout-year-there-was-idea-we-were.

Bechtol, Bruce E. Jr. "North Korea's Illegal Weapons Trade." *Foreign Affairs*. Jun 6, 2018. Retrieved from https://www.foreignaffairs.com/articles/north-korea/2018-06-06/north-koreas-illegal-weapons-trade.

Billock, Jennifer. "How Korea's Demilitarized Zone Became an Accidental Wildlife Paradise." *Smithsonian*. Smithsonian Institution. Feb 12, 2018. Retrieved from https://www.smithsonianmag.com/travel/wildlife-thrives-dmz-korea-risk-location-180967842/.

Boghani, Priyanka. "The U.S. and North Korea on the Brink: A Timeline." *Frontline*. PBS. Apr 18, 2018. Retrieved from https://www.pbs.org/wgbh/frontline/article/the-u-s-and-north-korea-on-the-brink-a-timeline/.

Cartwright, Mark. "Dangun." *Ancient History Encyclopedia*. Oct 20, 2016. Retrieved from https://www.ancient.eu/Dangun/.

Choe, Sang-Hun. "North and South Korea Set Bold Goals: A Final Peace and No Nuclear Arms." *The New York Times*. The New York Times Co. Apr 27, 2018. Retrieved from https://www.nytimes.com/2018/04/27/world/asia/north-korea-south-kim-jong-un.html.

"Cold War." *GWU*. Eleanor Roosevelt Papers Project. George Washington University. 2015. Retrieved from https://www2.gwu.edu/~erpapers/teachinger/glossary/cold-war.cfm.

Cumings, Bruce. *Korea's Place in the Sun*. New York: W.W. Norton & Company, 2005.

Eilperin, Juliet. "Days in the Life of Jay Kim in the U.S. House of Correction." *The Washington Post*. The Washington Post Co. May 22, 1998. Retrieved from https://www.washingtonpost.com/wp-srv/politics/campaigns/keyraces98/stories/ca052298.htm.

"Factbox: History of Failure: Efforts to Negotiate on North Korean Disarmament." *Reuters*. Reuters. Mar 6, 2018.

Fuchs, Chris. "Dan Koh's Family Taught Him Government 'Should Be a Force for Good.'" *NBC News*. NBC. May 16, 2018. Retrieved from https://www.nbcnews.com/news/asian-america/dan-koh-s-family-taught-him-government-should-be-force-n861476?icid=related.

Fuchs, Chris. "There Hasn't Been a Korean American in Congress Since 1999: Come November, There Could Be 4." *NBC News*. NBC. Aug 28, 2018. Retrieved from https://www.nbcnews.com/news/asian-america/there-hasn-t-been-korean-american-congress-1999-come-november-n904211.

Gambino, Lauren. "Donald Trump Boasts That His Nuclear Button Is Bigger Than Kim Jong-un's." *The Guardian*. The Guardian News and Media. Jan 3, 2018. Retrieved from https://www.theguardian.com/us-news/2018/jan/03/donald-trump-boasts-nuclear-button-bigger-kim-jong-un.

Gwertzman, Bernard. "U.S. Papers Tell of '53 Policy to Use A-Bomb in Korea." *The New York Times*. The New York Times Co. Jun 8, 1984. Retrieved from https://www.nytimes.com/1984/06/08/world/us-papers-tell-of-53-policy-to-use-a-bomb-in-korea.html.

Hancocks, Paula, Jake Kwon, and Joshua Berlinger. "North, South Korea Begin Demilitarizing 'Scariest Place on Earth.'" *CNN*. CNN. Oct 25, 2018. Retrieved from https://www.cnn.com/2018/10/25/asia/north-south-korea-dmz-intl/index.html.

Hancocks, Paula, and Taehoon Lee. "Checkpoints, Curfews and Barbed Wire: Life in the Village on North Korea's Doorstep." *CNN*. CNN. Sep 5, 2017. Retrieved from https://www.cnn.com/2017/09/05/asia/south-korea-dmz-village/index.html.

"Here's the Transcript of Trump's Press Conference After Meeting Kim Jong Un." *Market Watch*. MarketWatch Inc. June 12, 2018. Retrieved from https://www.marketwatch.com/story/heres-the-transcript-of-trumps-press-conference-after-meeting-kim-jong-un-2018-06-12.

Hern, Alex. "North Korea Is a Bigger Cyber-Attack Threat Than Russia, Says Expert." *The Guardian*. The Guardian News and Media. Feb 26, 2018. Retrieved from https://www.theguardian.com/technology/2018/feb/26/north-korea-cyber-attack-threat-russia.

"The History of Korea." *UCC*. University College Cork, Ireland. 2018. Retrieved from https://www.ucc.ie/en/asian/research/asi/korean/factsaboutkorea/thehistoryofkorea/.

Hwang, Kyung Moon. *A History of Korea*. New York: Palgrave Macmillan, 2017.

Kasulis, Kelly. "South Korea's Play Culture Is a Dark Symptom of Overwork." *QZ*. Quartz Media. Dec 31, 2017. Retrieved from https://qz.com/1168746/south-koreas-play-culture-is-a-dark-symptom-of-overwork/.

Kim, Jeongmin, and Josh Smith. "North Korea Media Says Denuclearization Includes Ending 'U.S. Nuclear Threat.'" *Reuters*. Reuters News Agency. Dec 20, 2018. Retrieved from https://www.reuters.com/article/us-northkorea-usa-denuclearisation/north-korea-media-says-denuclearization-includes-ending-u-s-nuclear-threat-idUSKCN1OJ0J1.

Kim, Min-Joo. "North Korea Rejects Denuclearization Unless U.S. 'Nuclear Threat' Is Eliminated." *The Washington Post*. The Washington Post Co. Dec 20, 2018. Retrieved from https://www.washingtonpost.com/world/asia_pacific/north-korea-rejects-denuclearization-unless-us-nuclear-threat-is-eliminated/2018/12/20/fc-f642a2-0438-11e9-b5df-5d3874f1ac36_story.html?utm_term=.2627043ee426.

"Koreans in the U.S. Fact Sheet." *Pew Social Trends*. Pew Research Center. Sep 8, 2017. Retrieved from http://www.pewsocialtrends.org/fact-sheet/asian-americans-koreans-in-the-u-s/.

La Shure, Charles. "Korean Mythology." *Pantheon*. Encyclopedia Mythica. Sep 29, 2018. Retrieved from https://pantheon.org/articles/k/korean_mythology.html.

Larmer, Brook. "South Korea's Most Dangerous Enemy: Demographics." *The New York Times Magazine*. Feb 20, 2018. Retrieved from https://www.nytimes.com/2018/02/20/magazine/south-koreas-most-dangerous-enemy-demographics.html.

Mahtani, Melissa. "North Korea Is 'a Cult' to Kim Jong Un, Undercover Reporter Says." *CNN*. CNN Politics. Aug 12, 2017. Retrieved from https://www.cnn.com/2017/08/12/politics/undercover-reporter-north-korea-cult-cnntv/index.html.

Mai-Duc, Christine. "A Young Kim Supporter Values Her 'Very Conservative' Viewpoints." *Los Angeles Times*. Nov 6, 2018. Retrieved from https://www.latimes.com/politics/la-na-pol-midterm-election-day-updates-a-kim-supporter-values-her-very-1541539603-htmlstory.html.

Mollman, Steve. "North Korea Is Sitting on Trillions of Dollars of Untapped Wealth, and Its Neighbors Want In." *QZ*. Quartz Media. Jun 15, 2017. Retrieved from https://qz.com/1004330/north-korea-is-sitting-on-trillions-of-dollars-on-untapped-wealth-and-its-neighbors-want-a-piece-of-it/.

Nakashima, Ellen, and Philip Rucker. "U.S. Declares North Korea Carried Out Massive WannaCry Cyberattack." *The Washington Post*. The Washington Post Co. Dec 19, 2017. Retrieved from https://www.washingtonpost.com/world/national-security/us-set-to-declare-north-korea-carried-out-massive-wannacry-cyber-attack/2017/12/18/509deb1c-e446-11e7-a65d-1ac0fd7f097e_story.html?noredirect=on&utm_term=.e36f96a97ba3.

Nemeth, David J. "The Geography of the Koreas." *Asia Society*. Center for Global Education. 2018. Retrieved from https://asiasociety.org/education/geography-koreas.

"North Korea Nuclear Timeline Fast Facts." *CNN*. CNN. Apr 3, 2018. Retrieved from https://www.cnn.com/2013/10/29/world/asia/north-korea-nuclear-timeline---fast-facts/index.html.

"North Korea Profile—Timeline." *BBC News*. BBC. June 13, 2018. Retrieved from https://www.bbc.com/news/world-asia-pacific-15278612.

"North Korean Nuclear Negotiations, 1985-2018." *CFR*. Council on Foreign Relations. 2018. Retrieved from https://www.cfr.org/timeline/north-korean-nuclear-negotiations.

"Nuclear." *NTI*. Nuclear Threat Initiative. Oct 2018. Retrieved from https://www.nti.org/learn/countries/north-korea/nuclear/.

"The Nuclear Non-Proliferation Treaty (NPT), 1968." *U.S. Department of State*. Office of the Historian. 2016. Retrieved from https://history.state.gov/milestones/1961-1968/npt.

Pappas, Stephanie. "7 Strange Cultural Facts About North Korea." *Live Science*. Purch. Apr 8, 2013. Retrieved from https://www.livescience.com/28528-7-cultural-facts-north-korea.html.

Payne, Ed. "World Leaders React to North Korea's Nuclear Test." *CNN*. CNN. Feb 12, 2013. Retrieved from https://www.cnn.com/2013/02/12/world/north-korea-nuclear-reax/.

Pollack, Jonathan D. "The Threat from North Korea." *Brookings*. Brookings Institution. Apr 24, 2017. Retrieved from https://www.brookings.edu/blog/unpacked/2017/04/24/the-threat-from-north-korea/.

Quinn, Ben. "Unicorn Lair 'Discovered' in North Korea." *The Guardian*. The Guardian News and Media. Nov 30, 2012. Retrieved from https://www.theguardian.com/world/2012/nov/30/unicorn-lair-discovered-north-korea.

Ramani, Samuel. "North Korea's Syrian Connection." *The Diplomat*. Feb 27, 2018. Retrieved from https://thediplomat.com/2018/02/north-koreas-syrian-connection/.

Rode, Erin. "Increasing Numbers of Korean Americans Are Identifying as Democrats." *USC Annenberg Media*. University of Southern California. Apr 28, 2018. Retrieved from http://www.uscannenbergmedia.com/2018/04/28/increasing-numbers-of-korean-americans-are-identifying-as-democrats/.

Sanger, David E., and William J. Broad. "Trump Inherits a Secret Cyberwar Against North Korean Missiles." *The New York Times*. Mar 4, 2017. Retrieved from https://www.nytimes.com/2017/03/04/world/asia/north-korea-missile-program-sabotage.html?module=inline.

Se-hwan, Bak. "South Koreans Work Second-Longest Hours in OECD for Below Average Pay." *The Korea Herald*. Korea Herald Corporation. Aug 17, 2017. Retrieved from http://www.koreaherald.com/view.php?ud=20170816000716.

Shang, Eva. "CEOs in the Making: The Youngest Asian-Americans in Tech." *NBC News*. NBC. Feb 22, 2016. Retrieved from https://www.nbcnews.com/news/asian-america/ceos-making-youngest-asian-americans-tech-n516691.

"Singapore Mud-Sling: Donald Trump vs. Kim Jong Un Insults." *NDTV*. NDTV. Jun 11, 2018. Retrieved from https://www.ndtv.com/world-news/singapore-mud-sling-trump-vs-kim-insults-1865752.

"South Korea—Timeline." *BBC News*. May 1, 2018. Retrieved from https://www.bbc.com/news/world-asia-pacific-15292674.

Szczepanski, Kallie. "South Korea—Facts and History." *ThoughtCo*. DotDash. Aug 21, 2017. Retrieved from https://www.thoughtco.com/south-korea-facts-and-history-195724.

"Treaty on the Non-Proliferation of Nuclear Weapons (NPT)." *UN*. United Nations Office for Disarmament Affairs. Retrieved from https://www.un.org/disarmament/wmd/nuclear/npt/.

Washburn, Taylor. "How an Ancient Kingdom Explains Today's China-Korea Relations." *The Atlantic*. The Atlantic Montly Group. Apr 15, 2013. Retrieved from https://www.theatlantic.com/china/archive/2013/04/how-an-ancient-kingdom-explains-todays-china-korea-relations/274986/.

"Why So Many Koreans Are Called Kim." *The Economist*. The Economist Newspaper. Sep 9, 2014. Retrieved from https://www.economist.com/the-economist-explains/2014/09/08/why-so-many-koreans-are-called-kim.

"World Outraged by North Korea's Latest Nuke Test." *CNN*. CNN. May 25, 2009. Retrieved from http://www.cnn.com/2009/WORLD/asiapcf/05/24/nkorea.nuclear/index.html?section=cnn_latest.

Yoon, Dasl, and Andrew Jeong. "If You Think North Korea Is a Wild Place, Check Out the DMZ." *The Wall Street Journal*. Dow Jones & Company. Dec 3, 2018. Retrieved from https://www.wsj.com/articles/cranes-vs-cranes-korean-dmz-development-poses-a-test-for-conservation-1543762801.

Zong, Jie, and Jeanne Batalova. "Korean Immigrants in the United States." *MPI*. Migration Policy Institute. Feb 8, 2017. Retrieved from https://www.migrationpolicy.org/article/korean-immigrants-united-states.

Websites

Brookings Institution
www.brookings.edu

The Brookings Institution is a nonprofit public policy think tank located in Washington, D.C. Brookings utilizes research and expertise from more than 300 experts in a variety of fields and provides research, data, and policy recommendations on a variety of domestic and foreign relations issues. Brookings has published numerous analytical articles examining various aspects of the US relationship with the Korean peninsula.

Council on Foreign Relations (CFR)
www.cfr.org

The Council on Foreign Relations in a nonpartisan, nonprofit think tank and publisher specializing in US relations with other countries. Founded in 1921, CFR supports a large number of studies and research programs around the country and provides background information on US foreign policy issues for students, politicians, and government officials.

The Diplomat
www.diplomat.com

The Diplomat is an online publication headquartered in Japan that provides news and analysis on a wide variety of issues impacting the Asia-Pacific region. It covers a number of issues related to the Korean Peninsula and the ongoing nuclear arms negotiations between Korea and other nations.

Donald Trump Presidential Website
www.whitehouse.gov/people/donald-j-trump/

Website for Donald Trump's presidency. Provides links to information released by the White House during the Trump administration, including information about Trump's foreign policy statements, policies, and aims.

National Association or Korean Americans (NAKA)
www.naka.org

The National Association of Korean Americans is an advocacy group, founded in 1994, and working to promote the welfare of Korean Americans in the United

States. The organization provides information about civil rights issues impacting Korean Americans and on issues pertaining to North and South Korea.

United Nations Office for Disarmament Affairs (UNODA)

www.un.org/disarmament/wmd/nuclear/npt/

The United Nations Office for Disarmament Affairs (UNODA) is the branch of the United Nations in charge of overseeing the Nuclear Non-Proliferation Treaty. UNODA presents information on a variety of international issues involving nuclear weapons development or disarmament, including the ongoing controversy regarding North Korea's nuclear weapon's program.

US Department of State (DOS)

www.state.gov

The United States Department of State is the branch of the US government charged with advising the present on international affairs and foreign policy. The DOS publishes fact sheets on US relations with other countries as an informational resource for students, professionals, and politicians. The DOS website has data on US relations with North Korea, South Korea, and on the history of US negotiations with the Korean nations.

United States Embassy & Consulate in Korea

Kr.usembassy.gov

Website for the US embassy and consulate in South Korea provides articles, press statements, and a variety of background information on US-Korean relations. Also provides updated information on policy regarding travel to Korea and news items related to North or South Korea or the Trump administration's policies with regard to the Korean peninsula.

Index